FERTILITY DIET

MAIN COURSE - 60+ Breakfast, Lunch, Dinner and Dessert Recipes for Fertility Diet

TABLE OF CONTENTS

BREAKFAST 7

BANANA PANCAKES 7

PEAR PANCAKES 9

CHERRIES PANCAKES 10

RAISIN PANCAKES 11

NUTS PANCAKES 12

GUAVA MUFFINS 13

POMEGRANATE MUFFINS 15

PAPAYA MUFFINS 17

PEACH MUFFINS 19

PLUM MUFFINS 21

SIMPLE MUFFINS 23

OMELETTE 25

ZUCCHINI OMELETTE 27

TOMATO OMELETTE 29

RED BELL PEPPER OMELETTE 31

BROCCOLI OMELETTE 33

AVOCADO TOAST 35

PUMPKIN FRENCH TOAST 36

COCONUT CHAI OATMEAL 37

CACAO GRANOLA PARFAIT 39

PEANUT BUTTER TOAST 40

LUNCH 42

SIMPLE PIZZA RECIPE 42

ZUCCHINI PIZZA 44

- BEANS FRITATTA 45
- SPINACH FRITATTA 47
- ASIAN GREENS FRITATTA 49
- SALAMI FRITATTA 51
- BROCCOLI FRITATTA 53
- VEGETARIAN CARBONARA 55
- KALE & QUINOA BOWL 57
- AVOCADO TOAST 59
- FIG & BRIE GRILLED CHEESE 60
- QUINOA AND LENTIL SALAD 61
- NUTTY SALAD 62
- FERTILITY SALAD 63
- FERTILITY SALAD 2 64
- SHRIMP SALAD 65
- ASPARAGUS SALAD 66
- STEAKD AND RYE SALAD 67
- TUNA SALAD 68
- CHICKEN FAJITA SALAD 69
- ***DINNER*** 71
- CAULIFLOWER RECIPE 71
- BROCCOLI RECIPE 73
- TOMATOES & HAM PIZZA 74
- CELERY SOUP 76
- BRUSSEL SPROUTS SOUP 78
- SPINACH SOUP 80
- CANTALOUPE SOUP 82

POTATO SOUP 84

SMOOTHIES.. 87

GINGER COLADA SMOOTHIE 87

RAINBOW SMOOTHIE... 88

ACAI SMOOTHIE 89

BERRY SMOOTHIE 90

GREEN SMOOTHIE 91

SUNRISE SMOOTHIE 92

SOY SMOOTHIE 93

POWER SMOOTHIE 94

OAT SMOOTHIE 95

APPLE SMOOTHIE 96

Copyright 2019 by Noah Jerris - All rights reserved.

This document is geared towards providing exact and reliable information in regards to the topic and issue covered. The publication is sold with the idea that the publisher is not required to render accounting, officially permitted, or otherwise, qualified services. If advice is necessary, legal or professional, a practiced individual in the profession should be ordered.

- From a Declaration of Principles which was accepted and approved equally by a Committee of the American Bar Association and a Committee of Publishers and Associations.

In no way is it legal to reproduce, duplicate, or transmit any part of this document in either electronic means or in printed format. Recording of this publication is strictly prohibited and any storage of this document is not allowed unless with written permission from the publisher. All rights reserved.

The information provided herein is stated to be truthful and consistent, in that any liability, in terms of inattention or otherwise, by any usage or abuse of any policies, processes, or directions contained within is the solitary and utter responsibility of the recipient reader. Under no circumstances will any legal responsibility or blame be held against the publisher for any reparation, damages, or monetary loss due to the information herein, either directly or indirectly.

Respective authors own all copyrights not held by the publisher.

The information herein is offered for informational

purposes solely, and is universal as so. The presentation of the information is without contract or any type of guarantee assurance.

The trademarks that are used are without any consent, and the publication of the trademark is without permission or backing by the trademark owner. All trademarks and brands within this book are for clarifying purposes only and are the owned by the owners themselves, not affiliated with this document.

Introduction

Fertility recipes for personal enjoyment but also for family enjoyment. You will love them for sure for how easy it is to prepare them.

BREAKFAST

BANANA PANCAKES

Serves: **4**

Prep Time: **10** Minutes

Cook Time: **20** Minutes

Total Time: **30** Minutes

INGREDIENTS

- 1 cup whole wheat flour
- ¼ tsp baking soda
- ¼ tsp baking powder
- 1 cup mashed banana
- 2 eggs
- 1 cup milk

DIRECTIONS

1. **In a bowl combine all ingredients together and mix well**
2. **In a skillet heat olive oil**

3. Pour ¼ of the batter and cook each pancake for 1-2 minutes per side
4. When ready remove from heat and serve

PEAR PANCAKES

Serves: **4**

Prep Time: **10** Minutes

Cook Time: **30** Minutes

Total Time: **40** Minutes

INGREDIENTS

- 1 cup whole wheat flour
- ¼ tsp baking soda
- ¼ tsp baking powder
- 1 cup pear
- 2 eggs
- 1 cup milk

DIRECTIONS

1. In a bowl combine all ingredients together and mix well
2. In a skillet heat olive oil
3. Pour ¼ of the batter and cook each pancake for 1-2 minutes per side
4. When ready remove from heat and serve

CHERRIES PANCAKES

Serves: **4**

Prep Time: **10** Minutes

Cook Time: **20** Minutes

Total Time: **30** Minutes

INGREDIENTS

- 1 cup whole wheat flour
- ¼ tsp baking soda
- ¼ tsp baking powder
- 1 cup cherries
- 2 eggs
- 1 cup milk

DIRECTIONS

1. In a bowl combine all ingredients together and mix well
2. In a skillet heat olive oil
3. Pour ¼ of the batter and cook each pancake for 1-2 minutes per side
4. When ready remove from heat and serve

RAISIN PANCAKES

Serves: *4*
Prep Time: *10* Minutes
Cook Time: *20* Minutes
Total Time: *30* Minutes

INGREDIENTS

- 1 cup whole wheat flour
- ¼ tsp baking soda
- ¼ tsp baking powder
- ½ cup raisins
- 2 eggs
- 1 cup milk

DIRECTIONS

1. In a bowl combine all ingredients together and mix well
2. In a skillet heat olive oil
3. Pour ¼ of the batter and cook each pancake for 1-2 minutes per side
4. When ready remove from heat and serve

NUTS PANCAKES

Serves: **4**

Prep Time: **10** Minutes

Cook Time: **30** Minutes

Total Time: **40** Minutes

INGREDIENTS

- 1 cup whole wheat flour
- ¼ tsp baking soda
- ¼ tsp baking powder
- 2 eggs
- 1 cup milk
- ½ cup nuts

DIRECTIONS

1. In a bowl combine all ingredients together and mix well
2. In a skillet heat olive oil
3. Pour ¼ of the batter and cook each pancake for 1-2 minutes per side
4. When ready remove from heat and serve

GUAVA MUFFINS

Serves: *8-12*
Prep Time: *10*   Minutes
Cook Time: *20*   Minutes
Total Time: *30*   Minutes

INGREDIENTS

- 2 eggs
- 1 tablespoon olive oil
- 1 cup milk
- 2 cups whole wheat flour
- 1 tsp baking soda
- ¼ tsp baking soda
- 1 cup guava
- 1 tsp cinnamon
- ¼ cup molasses

DIRECTIONS

1. In a bowl combine all dry ingredients
2. In another bowl combine all dry ingredients

3. Combine wet and dry ingredients together
4. Pour mixture into 8-12 prepared muffin cups, fill 2/3 of the cups
5. Bake for 18-20 minutes at 375 F
6. When ready remove from the oven and serve

POMEGRANATE MUFFINS

Serves: *8-12*
Prep Time: *10* Minutes
Cook Time: *20* Minutes
Total Time: *30* Minutes

INGREDIENTS

- 2 eggs
- 1 tablespoon olive oil
- 1 cup milk
- 2 cups whole wheat flour
- 1 tsp baking soda
- ¼ tsp baking soda
- 1 tsp cinnamon
- 1 cup mashed pomegranate

DIRECTIONS

1. In a bowl combine all dry ingredients
2. In another bowl combine all dry ingredients
3. Combine wet and dry ingredients together

4. Pour mixture into 8-12 prepared muffin cups, fill 2/3 of the cups
5. Bake for 18-20 minutes at 375 F
6. When ready remove from the oven and serve

PAPAYA MUFFINS

Serves: **8-12**
Prep Time: **10** Minutes
Cook Time: **20** Minutes
Total Time: **30** Minutes

INGREDIENTS

- 2 eggs
- 1 tablespoon olive oil
- 1 cup milk
- 2 cups whole wheat flour
- 1 tsp baking soda
- ¼ tsp baking soda
- 1 tsp cinnamon
- 1 cup papaya

DIRECTIONS

1. In a bowl combine all dry ingredients
2. In another bowl combine all dry ingredients
3. Combine wet and dry ingredients together

4. Pour mixture into 8-12 prepared muffin cups, fill 2/3 of the cups
5. Bake for 18-20 minutes at 375 F
6. When ready remove from the oven and serve

PEACH MUFFINS

Serves: *8-12*

Prep Time: *10* Minutes

Cook Time: *20* Minutes

Total Time: *30* Minutes

INGREDIENTS

- 2 eggs
- 1 tablespoon olive oil
- 1 cup milk
- 2 cups whole wheat flour
- 1 tsp baking soda
- ¼ tsp baking soda
- 1 tsp cinnamon
- 1 cup peach

DIRECTIONS

1. In a bowl combine all dry ingredients
2. In another bowl combine all dry ingredients
3. Combine wet and dry ingredients together

4. Pour mixture into 8-12 prepared muffin cups, fill 2/3 of the cups
5. Bake for 18-20 minutes at 375 F
6. When ready remove from the oven and serve

PLUM MUFFINS

Serves: **8-12**
Prep Time: **10** Minutes
Cook Time: **20** Minutes
Total Time: **30** Minutes

INGREDIENTS

- 2 eggs
- 1 tablespoon olive oil
- 1 cup milk
- 2 cups whole wheat flour
- 1 tsp baking soda
- ¼ tsp baking soda
- 1 tsp cinnamon
- 1 cup plums

DIRECTIONS

1. In a bowl combine all dry ingredients
2. In another bowl combine all dry ingredients
3. Combine wet and dry ingredients together

4. Pour mixture into 8-12 prepared muffin cups, fill 2/3 of the cups
5. Bake for 18-20 minutes at 375 F
6. When ready remove from the oven and serve

SIMPLE MUFFINS

Serves: **8-12**

Prep Time: **10** Minutes

Cook Time: **20** Minutes

Total Time: **30** Minutes

INGREDIENTS

- 2 eggs
- 1 tablespoon olive oil
- 1 cup milk
- 2 cups whole wheat flour
- 1 tsp baking soda
- ¼ tsp baking soda
- 1 tsp cinnamon

DIRECTIONS

1. In a bowl combine all dry ingredients
2. In another bowl combine all dry ingredients
3. Combine wet and dry ingredients together

4. Pour mixture into 8-12 prepared muffin cups, fill 2/3 of the cups
5. Bake for 18-20 minutes at 375 F
6. When ready remove from the oven and serve

OMELETTE

Serves: **1**

Prep Time: **5** Minutes

Cook Time: **10** Minutes

Total Time: **15** Minutes

INGREDIENTS

- 2 eggs
- ¼ tsp salt
- ¼ tsp black pepper
- 1 tablespoon olive oil
- ¼ cup cheese
- ¼ tsp basil

DIRECTIONS

1. **In a bowl combine all ingredients together and mix well**
2. **In a skillet heat olive oil and pour the egg mixture**
3. **Cook for 1-2 minutes per side**

4. When ready remove omelette from the skillet and serve

ZUCCHINI OMELETTE

Serves: **1**

Prep Time: **5** Minutes

Cook Time: **10** Minutes

Total Time: **15** Minutes

INGREDIENTS

- 2 eggs
- ¼ tsp salt
- ¼ tsp black pepper
- 1 tablespoon olive oil
- ¼ cup cheese
- ¼ tsp basil
- 1 cup zucchini

DIRECTIONS

1. **In a bowl combine all ingredients together and mix well**
2. **In a skillet heat olive oil and pour the egg mixture**
3. **Cook for 1-2 minutes per side**

4. When ready remove omelette from the skillet and serve

TOMATO OMELETTE

Serves: **1**

Prep Time: **5** Minutes

Cook Time: **10** Minutes

Total Time: **15** Minutes

INGREDIENTS

- 2 eggs
- ¼ tsp salt
- ¼ tsp black pepper
- 1 tablespoon olive oil
- ¼ cup cheese
- ¼ tsp basil
- 1 cup red onion
- 1 tomato

DIRECTIONS

1. In a bowl combine all ingredients together and mix well
2. In a skillet heat olive oil and pour the egg mixture

3. Cook for 1-2 minutes per side
4. When ready remove omelette from the skillet and serve

RED BELL PEPPER OMELETTE

Serves: **1**

Prep Time: **5** Minutes

Cook Time: **10** Minutes

Total Time: **15** Minutes

INGREDIENTS

- 2 eggs
- ¼ tsp salt
- ¼ tsp black pepper
- 1 tablespoon olive oil
- ¼ cup cheese
- ¼ tsp basil
- 1 cup red bell pepper

DIRECTIONS

1. In a bowl combine all ingredients together and mix well
2. In a skillet heat olive oil and pour the egg mixture
3. Cook for 1-2 minutes per side

4. When ready remove omelette from the skillet and serve

BROCCOLI OMELETTE

Serves: **1**
Prep Time: **5** Minutes
Cook Time: **10** Minutes
Total Time: **15** Minutes

INGREDIENTS

- 2 eggs
- ¼ tsp salt
- ¼ tsp black pepper
- 1 tablespoon olive oil
- ¼ cup cheese
- ¼ tsp basil
- 1 cup braccoli

DIRECTIONS

1. In a bowl combine all ingredients together and mix well
2. In a skillet heat olive oil and pour the egg mixture
3. Cook for 1-2 minutes per side

4. When ready remove omelette from the skillet and serve

AVOCADO TOAST

Serves: **2**

Prep Time: **5** Minutes

Cook Time: **5** Minutes

Total Time: **10** Minutes

INGREDIENTS

- 4 slices bread
- 1 avocado
- ¼ tsp red chili flakes
- ¼ tsp salt

DIRECTIONS

1. **Toast the bread and set aside**
2. **Lay avocado slices on each bread slice**
3. **Sprinkle with red chili flakes and salt**
4. **Serve when ready**

PUMPKIN FRENCH TOAST

Serves: **3**

Prep Time: **5** Minutes

Cook Time: **15** Minutes

Total Time: **20** Minutes

INGREDIENTS

- ¼ cup milk
- 2 eggs
- ½ cup pumpkin puree
- 1 tablespoon pumpkin slice
- 6 bread slices

DIRECTIONS

1. In a bowl whisk all ingredients for the dipping
2. Dip the bread into the dipping and let it soak for 3-4 minutes
3. In a skillet heat olive oil and fry each slice for 2-3 minutes per side
4. When ready remove from the skillet and serve

COCONUT CHAI OATMEAL

Serves: 2
Prep Time: 5 Minutes
Cook Time: 15 Minutes
Total Time: 20 Minutes

INGREDIENTS

- ¼ cup oats
- ½ cup chia tea
- ¼ cup coconut milk
- 1 peach
- ¼ tsp coconut oil
- 1 tsp coconut flakes

DIRECTIONS

1. In a bowl combine together oats, coconut milk, chia tea and microwave until thickness
2. In a saucepan add peach slices and cook for 2-3 minutes
3. Place peaches over the oats and top with coconut flakes

4. Serve when ready

CACAO GRANOLA PARFAIT

Serves: **4**
Prep Time: **10** Minutes
Cook Time: **30** Minutes
Total Time: **40** Minutes

INGREDIENTS

- 4 oz. coconut yogurt
- ¼ cup gluten-free granola
- 1 tablespoon cacao nibs
- 1 oz. raspberries

DIRECTIONS

1. Place all ingredients in a bowl and mix well
2. Serve when ready

PEANUT BUTTER TOAST

Serves: **1**
Prep Time: **5** Minutes
Cook Time: **5** Minutes
Total Time: **10** Minutes

INGREDIENTS

- 2 slices gluten-free toast
- 2 tablespoons peanut butter
- ¼ tsp flax seeds
- ¼ tsp chia seeds

DIRECTIONS

1. Place all ingredients in a bowl and mix well
2. Serve when ready

LUNCH

SIMPLE PIZZA RECIPE

Serves: **6-8**

Prep Time: **10** Minutes

Cook Time: **15** Minutes

Total Time: **25** Minutes

INGREDIENTS

- 1 pizza crust
- ½ cup tomato sauce
- ¼ black pepper
- 1 cup pepperoni slices
- 1 cup mozzarella cheese
- 1 cup olives

DIRECTIONS

1. Spread tomato sauce on the pizza crust
2. Place all the toppings on the pizza crust
3. Bake the pizza at 425 F for 12-15 minutes

4. **When ready remove pizza from the oven and serve**

ZUCCHINI PIZZA

Serves: **6-8**

Prep Time: **10** Minutes

Cook Time: **15** Minutes

Total Time: **25** Minutes

INGREDIENTS

- 1 pizza crust
- ½ cup tomato sauce
- ¼ black pepper
- 1 cup zucchini slices
- 1 cup mozzarella cheese
- 1 cup olives

DIRECTIONS

1. Spread tomato sauce on the pizza crust
2. Place all the toppings on the pizza crust
3. Bake the pizza at 425 F for 12-15 minutes
4. When ready remove pizza from the oven and serve

BEANS FRITATTA

Serves: **2**

Prep Time: **10** Minutes

Cook Time: **20** Minutes

Total Time: **30** Minutes

INGREDIENTS

- ½ lb. black beans
- 1 tablespoon olive oil
- ½ red onion
- ¼ tsp salt
- 2 eggs
- 2 oz. cheddar cheese
- 1 garlic clove
- ¼ tsp dill

DIRECTIONS

1. In a bowl whisk eggs with salt and cheese
2. In a frying pan heat olive oil and pour egg mixture

3. Add remaining ingredients and mix well
4. Serve when ready

SPINACH FRITATTA

Serves: 2

Prep Time: 10 Minutes

Cook Time: 20 Minutes

Total Time: 30 Minutes

INGREDIENTS

- ½ lb. spinach
- 1 tablespoon olive oil
- ½ red onion
- ¼ tsp salt
- 2 eggs
- 2 oz. cheddar cheese
- 1 garlic clove
- ¼ tsp dill

DIRECTIONS

1. In a bowl whisk eggs with salt and cheese
2. In a frying pan heat olive oil and pour egg mixture

3. Add remaining ingredients and mix well
4. Serve when ready

ASIAN GREENS FRITATTA

Serves: **2**
Prep Time: **10** Minutes
Cook Time: **20** Minutes
Total Time: **30** Minutes

INGREDIENTS

- 1 cup Asian greens
- 1 tablespoon olive oil
- ½ red onion
- ¼ tsp salt
- 2 eggs
- 2 oz. cheddar cheese
- 1 garlic clove
- ¼ tsp dill

DIRECTIONS

1. In a bowl whisk eggs with salt and cheese
2. In a frying pan heat olive oil and pour egg mixture

3. Add remaining ingredients and mix well
4. Serve when ready

SALAMI FRITATTA

Serves: **2**
Prep Time: **10** Minutes
Cook Time: **20** Minutes
Total Time: **30** Minutes

INGREDIENTS

- 8-10 slices salami
- 1 tablespoon olive oil
- ½ red onion
- ¼ tsp salt
- 2 eggs
- 2 oz. parmesan cheese
- 1 garlic clove
- ¼ tsp dill

DIRECTIONS

1. In a bowl whisk eggs with salt and parmesan cheese
2. In a frying pan heat olive oil and pour egg mixture

3. Add remaining ingredients and mix well
4. When salami and eggs are cooked remove from heat and serve

BROCCOLI FRITATTA

Serves: **2**
Prep Time: **10** Minutes
Cook Time: **20** Minutes
Total Time: **30** Minutes

INGREDIENTS

- 1 cup broccoli
- 2 eggs
- 1 tablespoon olive oil
- ½ red onion
- ¼ tsp salt
- 2 oz. cheddar cheese
- 1 garlic clove
- ¼ tsp dill

DIRECTIONS

1. In a bowl whisk eggs with salt and cheese
2. In a frying pan heat olive oil and pour egg mixture

3. Add remaining ingredients and mix well
4. Serve when ready

VEGETARIAN CARBONARA

Serves: **2**

Prep Time: **10** Minutes

Cook Time: **20** Minutes

Total Time: **30** Minutes

INGREDIENTS

- ¼ cup olive oil
- 1 tablespoon Worcestershire sauce
- 1 garlic clove
- 15 oz. spaghetti
- 1 cup water
- 2 eggs
- 1 tsp salt
- ½ cup parmesan cheese

DIRECTIONS

1. In a pot boil spaghetti until al dente
2. In another bowl whisk eggs with salt

3. Whisk ¼ cup pasta with egg mixture, garlic and pour a Dutch oven
4. When ready remove to a plate, add parmesan cheese and serve

KALE & QUINOA BOWL

Serves: **2**

Prep Time: **10** Minutes

Cook Time: **20** Minutes

Total Time: **30** Minutes

INGREDIENTS

- 1 cup cooked quinoa
- 1 bunch kale
- 2 tablespoons olive oil
- 1 cup tomatoes
- Juice from ½ lemon
- ¼ cup parmesan cheese

DIRECTIONS

1. Set cooked quinoa aside
2. In a pan heat olive oil and add kale
3. Add water and cook until tender
4. Place the cooked kale in a bowl
5. Add quinoa, tomatoes and lemon juice

6. Top with parmesan cheese and serve

AVOCADO TOAST

Serves: **1**

Prep Time: **5** Minutes

Cook Time: **5** Minutes

Total Time: **10** Minutes

INGREDIENTS

- 2 slices gluten free toast
- 1 avocado
- 1 cup smoked salmon
- 6-8 basil leaves
- ¼ tsp salt

DIRECTIONS

1. **Top bread with avocado and salmon**
2. **Add basil leaves, salt and top with another bread slice**
3. **Serve when ready**

FIG & BRIE GRILLED CHEESE

Serves: **2**

Prep Time: **10** Minutes

Cook Time: **10** Minutes

Total Time: **20** Minutes

INGREDIENTS

- 1 tablespoon butter
- 4 slices bread
- 6 oz. brie cheese
- 2 figs

DIRECTIONS

1. In a pan heat olive oil
2. Divide the figs and cheese between 2 bread slices
3. Top with the other bread slices
4. Place in the pan and cover with a lid
5. Cook for 3-4 minutes per side on low heat
6. When ready remove from heat and serve

QUINOA AND LENTIL SALAD

Serves: 2
Prep Time: 5 Minutes
Cook Time: 5 Minutes
Total Time: 10 Minutes

INGREDIENTS

- 1 cup cooked lentils
- 1 tsp salt
- 1 cup cooked quinoa
- 2 tablespoons olive oil
- 1 tsp salt
- 1 tomato
- 1 avocado
- 1 tsp cilantro

DIRECTIONS

1. In a bowl mix all ingredients and mix well
2. Serve with dressing

NUTTY SALAD

Serves: **2**

Prep Time: **5** Minutes

Cook Time: **5** Minutes

Total Time: **10** Minutes

INGREDIENTS

- 1 cup cooked quinoa
- 2 stalks celery
- 1 roasted capsicum
- ¼ cup cranberries
- ¼ cup almonds
- ½ cup walnuts
- ¼ red onion

DIRECTIONS

1. In a bowl mix all ingredients and mix well
2. Serve with dressing

FERTILITY SALAD

Serves: 2
Prep Time: 5 Minutes
Cook Time: 5 Minutes
Total Time: **10** Minutes

INGREDIENTS

- 1 cup romaine lettuce
- 1 cup roasted chicken
- 1 avocado
- 1 cup Goji berries
- 2 cups olives
- 1 pinch salt

DIRECTIONS

1. In a bowl mix all ingredients and mix well
2. Serve with dressing

FERTILITY SALAD 2

Serves: 2
Prep Time: 5 Minutes
Cook Time: 5 Minutes
Total Time: 10 Minutes

INGREDIENTS

- 1 cup chard
- 1 cup spinach
- 1 cup broccoli
- 2 cups cooked lentils
- ½ cup walnuts
- 1 cup berries
- 1 cup lemon salad dressing

DIRECTIONS

1. **In a bowl mix all ingredients and mix well**
2. **Serve with dressing**

SHRIMP SALAD

Serves: 2

Prep Time: 5 Minutes

Cook Time: 5 Minutes

Total Time: 10 Minutes

INGREDIENTS

- 8 oz. shrimp
- 1 avocado
- 1 cucumber
- 2 tomatoes
- handful of cilantro leaves
- 1 cup salad dressing

DIRECTIONS

1. In a bowl mix all ingredients and mix well
2. Serve with dressing

ASPARAGUS SALAD

Serves: **2**

Prep Time: **5** Minutes

Cook Time: **5** Minutes

Total Time: **10** Minutes

INGREDIENTS

- 1 cup asparagus
- ½ cup Parmesan cheese
- ¼ cup mustard
- ¼ cup olive oil
- 1 cucumber

DIRECTIONS

1. **In a bowl mix all ingredients and mix well**
2. **Serve with dressing**

STEAKD AND RYE SALAD

Serves: 2
Prep Time: 5 Minutes
Cook Time: 5 Minutes
Total Time: 10 Minutes

INGREDIENTS

- 2 tsp red wine vinegar
- 2 tablespoons olive oil
- 2 cloves garlic
- 1 bulb fennel
- 1 onion
- 4 slices rye bread
- 1 lb. sirloin steak

DIRECTIONS

1. In a bowl mix all ingredients and mix well
2. Serve with dressing

TUNA SALAD

Serves: 2
Prep Time: 5 Minutes
Cook Time: 5 Minutes
Total Time: 10 Minutes

INGREDIENTS

- 10 oz. green beans
- 1 shallot
- 1 cup basil leaves
- 1 tablespoon olive oil
- 2 cups leaf lettuce
- 1 cup black beans
- 2 cans tuna

DIRECTIONS

1. In a bowl mix all ingredients and mix well
2. Serve with dressing

CHICKEN FAJITA SALAD

Serves: **2**

Prep Time: **5** Minutes

Cook Time: **5** Minutes

Total Time: **10** Minutes

INGREDIENTS

- 2 cups cooked chicken breast
- 2 peppers
- 1 jalapeno
- 1 onion
- 2 tablespoons olive oil
- 1 avocado
- 1 tsp honey
- 1 cup cilantro

DIRECTIONS

1. **In a bowl mix all ingredients and mix well**
2. **Serve with dressing**

DINNER

CAULIFLOWER RECIPE

Serves: **6-8**
Prep Time: **10** Minutes
Cook Time: **15** Minutes
Total Time: **25** Minutes

INGREDIENTS

- 1 pizza crust
- ½ cup tomato sauce
- ¼ black pepper
- 1 cup cauliflower
- 1 cup mozzarella cheese
- 1 cup olives

DIRECTIONS

1. Spread tomato sauce on the pizza crust
2. Place all the toppings on the pizza crust
3. Bake the pizza at 425 F for 12-15 minutes

4. When ready remove pizza from the oven and serve

BROCCOLI RECIPE

Serves: **6-8**

Prep Time: **10** Minutes

Cook Time: **15** Minutes

Total Time: **25** Minutes

INGREDIENTS

- 1 pizza crust
- ½ cup tomato sauce
- ¼ black pepper
- 1 cup broccoli
- 1 cup mozzarella cheese
- 1 cup olives

DIRECTIONS

1. Spread tomato sauce on the pizza crust
2. Place all the toppings on the pizza crust
3. Bake the pizza at 425 F for 12-15 minutes
4. When ready remove pizza from the oven and serve

TOMATOES & HAM PIZZA

Serves: **6-8**

Prep Time: **10** Minutes

Cook Time: **15** Minutes

Total Time: **25** Minutes

INGREDIENTS

- 1 pizza crust
- ½ cup tomato sauce
- ¼ black pepper
- 1 cup pepperoni slices
- 1 cup tomatoes
- 6-8 ham slices
- 1 cup mozzarella cheese
- 1 cup olives

DIRECTIONS

1. **Spread tomato sauce on the pizza crust**
2. **Place all the toppings on the pizza crust**
3. **Bake the pizza at 425 F for 12-15 minutes**

4. When ready remove pizza from the oven and serve

CELERY SOUP

Serves: **4**

Prep Time: **10** Minutes

Cook Time: **20** Minutes

Total Time: **30** Minutes

INGREDIENTS

- 1 tablespoon olive oil
- 1 lb. celery
- ¼ red onion
- ½ cup all-purpose flour
- ¼ tsp salt
- ¼ tsp pepper
- 1 can vegetable broth
- 1 cup heavy cream

DIRECTIONS

1. In a saucepan heat olive oil and sauté onion until tender
2. Add remaining ingredients to the saucepan and bring to a boil

3. When all the vegetables are tender transfer to a blender and blend until smooth
4. Pour soup into bowls, garnish with parsley and serve

BRUSSEL SPROUTS SOUP

Serves: **4**

Prep Time: **10** Minutes

Cook Time: **20** Minutes

Total Time: **30** Minutes

INGREDIENTS

- 1 tablespoon olive oil
- 1 lb. brussel sprouts
- ¼ red onion
- ½ cup all-purpose flour
- ¼ tsp salt
- ¼ tsp pepper
- 1 can vegetable broth
- 1 cup heavy cream

DIRECTIONS

1. In a saucepan heat olive oil and sauté zucchini until tender
2. Add remaining ingredients to the saucepan and bring to a boil

3. When all the vegetables are tender transfer to a blender and blend until smooth
4. Pour soup into bowls, garnish with parsley and serve

SPINACH SOUP

Serves: **4**

Prep Time: **10** Minutes

Cook Time: **20** Minutes

Total Time: **30** Minutes

INGREDIENTS

- 1 tablespoon olive oil
- 1 lb. spinach
- ¼ red onion
- ½ cup all-purpose flour
- ¼ tsp salt
- ¼ tsp pepper
- 1 can vegetable broth
- 1 cup heavy cream

DIRECTIONS

1. In a saucepan heat olive oil and sauté spinach until tender
2. Add remaining ingredients to the saucepan and bring to a boil

3. When all the vegetables are tender transfer to a blender and blend until smooth
4. Pour soup into bowls, garnish with parsley and serve

CANTALOUPE SOUP

Serves: **4**

Prep Time: **10** Minutes

Cook Time: **20** Minutes

Total Time: **30** Minutes

INGREDIENTS

- 1 tablespoon olive oil
- 1 lb. cantaloupe
- ¼ red onion
- ½ cup all-purpose flour
- ¼ tsp salt
- ¼ tsp pepper
- 1 can vegetable broth
- 1 cup heavy cream

DIRECTIONS

1. In a saucepan heat olive oil and sauté onion until tender
2. Add remaining ingredients to the saucepan and bring to a boil

3. When all the vegetables are tender transfer to a blender and blend until smooth
4. Pour soup into bowls, garnish with parsley and serve

POTATO SOUP

Serves: **4**

Prep Time: **10** Minutes

Cook Time: **20** Minutes

Total Time: **30** Minutes

INGREDIENTS

- 1 tablespoon olive oil
- 1 lb. mushrooms
- ¼ red onion
- ½ cup all-purpose flour
- ¼ tsp salt
- ¼ tsp pepper
- 1 can vegetable broth
- 1 cup heavy cream

DIRECTIONS

1. In a saucepan heat olive oil and sauté potatoes until tender
2. Add remaining ingredients to the saucepan and bring to a boil

3. When all the vegetables are tender transfer to a blender and blend until smooth
4. Pour soup into bowls, garnish with parsley and serve

SMOOTHIES

GINGER COLADA SMOOTHIE

Serves: **1**
Prep Time: **5** Minutes
Cook Time: **5** Minutes
Total Time: **10** Minutes

INGREDIENTS

- 1 tablespoon ginger
- ½ cup lemon juice
- 1 cup pineapple
- 1 banana
- 1 handful spinach
- 1 handful kale
- 1 cup ice

DIRECTIONS

1. **In a blender place all ingredients and blend until smooth**
2. **Pour smoothie in a glass and serve**

RAINBOW SMOOTHIE

Serves: **1**

Prep Time: **5** Minutes

Cook Time: **5** Minutes

Total Time: **10** Minutes

INGREDIENTS

- ¼ cup grapefruit
- ¼ cup watermelon
- 1 cup raspberries
- 1 cup pomegranate
- 1 cup ice

DIRECTIONS

1. In a blender place all ingredients and blend until smooth
2. Pour smoothie in a glass and serve

ACAI SMOOTHIE

Serves: **1**

Prep Time: **5** Minutes

Cook Time: **5** Minutes

Total Time: **10** Minutes

INGREDIENTS

- 1 cup acai puree
- 1 banana
- 1 cup pomegranate juice
- 1 kiwi
- ½ lemon

DIRECTIONS

1. **In a blender place all ingredients and blend until smooth**
2. **Pour smoothie in a glass and serve**

BERRY SMOOTHIE

Serves: **1**

Prep Time: **5** Minutes

Cook Time: **5** Minutes

Total Time: **10** Minutes

INGREDIENTS

- 1 cup strawberries
- 1 cup blueberries
- ½ cup orange juice
- ½ cup coconut water
- 1 cup ice

DIRECTIONS

1. **In a blender place all ingredients and blend until smooth**
2. **Pour smoothie in a glass and serve**

GREEN SMOOTHIE

Serves: **1**

Prep Time: **5** Minutes

Cook Time: **5** Minutes

Total Time: **10** Minutes

INGREDIENTS

- 2 stalks celery
- 4 cups spinach
- 1 pear
- 1 banana
- 1 tablespoon lime juice
- 1 cup coconut water
- 1 cup ice

DIRECTIONS

1. In a blender place all ingredients and blend until smooth
2. Pour smoothie in a glass and serve

SUNRISE SMOOTHIE

Serves: *1*

Prep Time: *5* Minutes

Cook Time: *5* Minutes

Total Time: *10* Minutes

INGREDIENTS

- 2 cups kiwi
- 2 bananas
- 2 mangoes
- ½ cup pineapple
- 1 cup ice
- 1 cup coconut water
- 1 tablespoon honey

DIRECTIONS

1. In a blender place all ingredients and blend until smooth
2. Pour smoothie in a glass and serve

SOY SMOOTHIE

Serves: **1**

Prep Time: **5** Minutes

Cook Time: **5** Minutes

Total Time: **10** Minutes

INGREDIENTS

- 2 cups blueberries
- 1 cup soy vanilla yogurt
- 1 cup soy milk
- 1 tsp vanilla essence

DIRECTIONS

1. **In a blender place all ingredients and blend until smooth**
2. **Pour smoothie in a glass and serve**

POWER SMOOTHIE

Serves: **1**
Prep Time: **5** Minutes
Cook Time: **5** Minutes
Total Time: **10** Minutes

INGREDIENTS

- 1 cup kale
- ¼ cup greens
- ¼ cup baby spinach
- ¼ cup greens
- ½ cup pineapple
- ½ cup blueberries
- 1 cup almon milk

DIRECTIONS

1. **In a blender place all ingredients and blend until smooth**
2. **Pour smoothie in a glass and serve**

OAT SMOOTHIE

Serves: **1**

Prep Time: **5** Minutes

Cook Time: **5** Minutes

Total Time: **10** Minutes

INGREDIENTS

- 1 cup orange juice
- ¼ cup oats
- 1 tablespoon flaxseed meal
- 1 tablespoon honey
- 1 banana
- 1 cup ice

DIRECTIONS

1. In a blender place all ingredients and blend until smooth
2. Pour smoothie in a glass and serve

APPLE SMOOTHIE

Serves: **1**

Prep Time: **5** Minutes

Cook Time: **5** Minutes

Total Time: **10** Minutes

INGREDIENTS

- 2 green apples
- 1 banana
- ½ cup almond milk
- 1 cup ice
- ¼ cup vanilla yogurt
- 1 tsp cinnamon
- ¼ tsp nutmeg

DIRECTIONS

1. In a blender place all ingredients and blend until smooth
2. Pour smoothie in a glass and serve

THANK YOU FOR READING THIS BOOK!

Printed in Great Britain
by Amazon

CONTENT

Introduction _____ 1

PART 1: WHY EMPLOYEE ADVOCACY _____ 4
CHAPTER 1: Increasing the company's sales and profits _____ 8
CHAPTER 2: Building a happier company culture _____ 27
CHAPTER 3: Promoting thought leadership among the employees __ 41

PART 2: LAYING THE FOUNDATIONS _____ 46
CHAPTER 4: Creating and growing a powerful company page _____ 49
CHAPTER 5: Content strategy for the company page _____ 59
CHAPTER 6: Getting the company ready and excited to start _____ 69

PART 3: TRAINING THE TEAMS _____ 86
CHAPTER 7: Employees' personal profiles _____ 88
CHAPTER 8: Creating content on personal profiles _____ 98
CHAPTER 9: Increasing the reach of the company page posts _____ 109
CHAPTER 10: Outreach and Social selling _____ 115

PART 4: MAXIMISING THE INVESTMENT _____ 132
CHAPTER 11: Steps to ensure the success of the programme _____ 134
CHAPTER 12: Measuring and monitoring success _____ 145
The End - or is this the beginning? _____ 161
Closing note _____ 162
The story of this book & acknowledgements _____ 163
About the author _____ 165
References _____ 167

I dedicate this book to all CEOs out there who know the struggle involved in getting their voices, and those of their companies, heard in the huge sea of communication that we know as 'the internet'.

I hope this book gives you the knowledge and the confidence to think differently and try new strategies.

Copyright 2024 ©Sarah Clay

All rights reserved. No part of this publication may be reproduced, stored in or introduced into a retrieval system, or transmitted, in any form, or by any means (electronical, mechanical, photocopying, recording or otherwise) without prior written permission from both the publisher and the copyright owner of this book.

This book is sold subject to the condition that it shall not, by way of trade or otherwise, be lent, resold, hired out, or otherwise circulated without the consent of the copyright owner in any form of binding or cover other than that in which it is published and without a similar condition including this condition being imposed on the subsequent purchaser.

First published in Great Britain in 2024

ISBN:
Paperback: 9798325485367
Hardcover: 9798327405233

Book coach: Malene Bendtsen
Cover design & layout: BookCoverHub

Website www.sarahclaysocial.com

LinkedIn is the registered trademark of LinkedIn Corporation or its affiliates. The use of the LinkedIn trademark in connection with this product does not signify any affiliation with or endorsement by LinkedIn Corporation or its affiliates.

EMPLOYEE ADVOCACY ON LINKEDIN®

How to use LinkedIn to build a **thriving** company culture, empower your team and **grow** your business

SARAH CLAY

This book is about how using a system of employee advocacy can lead to a happier company culture, lower staff turnover, and increased sales. The focus is on LinkedIn, simply because LinkedIn drives more B2B sales than any other social media platform.

Introduction

A big problem which many companies face is inconsistency of sales. World events, political shifts and economic downturns all play a part in a company's revenue. Companies of all sizes are also experiencing significant challenges regarding the happiness and loyalty of customers and employees. It's time to take action to solve these problems, and LinkedIn is a place to do this.

On the employee side, phenomena like 'quiet quitting' and 'the great resignation' are real threats to the culture of a company - and of course it's profits. In 2023, employee turnover rates in the UK increased to 13.7%[1] and are estimated to increase even more in 2024. With an average employee turnover cost amounting to 20% of the employee's salary, any sensible company would want to examine and implement strategies for keeping turnover as low as possible.

Another dramatic change is buying behaviour. People don't want to be 'sold' to, and bombarding consumers with salesy messages and content on social channels no longer works. The social platforms are meant to be social, and using them for selling is more complicated than ever before.

On the flip side, with the growth of social media channels, companies also have bigger opportunities than they have ever known to reach people far beyond their own network.

What many haven't realised is how well suited LinkedIn is to solve these problems. LinkedIn has seen huge changes recently. It is no longer just a CV database. It is a social information network where people communicate, exchange information, and build connections internally and externally. It's the biggest networking party in the world, it's open 24 hours a day, and it's free!

People join LinkedIn to expand their professional network and create opportunities for a better future, for themselves and for companies they support. This means LinkedIn users are open to new connections, and make an effort to find and create meaningful relationships to lead to business growth. With over a billion users, the potential for doing so is almost unlimited.

Employee advocacy has been around for many years although it probably didn't have a name when it first started being something companies were doing. The way we communicate now is constantly changing. People's individual voices are becoming stronger, whatever their role in a company. With remote and hybrid working now the norm in most organisations, colleagues have much less interaction with their peers and bosses. Some of you reading this will have colleagues you've never met in person. Whatever the reasons, employee advocacy is an effective new way to market ourselves and our companies and for now at least, it's here to stay.

This book will help you understand what employee advocacy is, why it is something for you to consider for your company and how to get started.

In this book, you will get answers to questions like these:

- What is employee advocacy?
- What might an employee advocacy scheme look like in your business?
- What are the critical factors in implementing a system of employee advocacy in your company?
- What kind of results can we expect to see with a properly implemented and managed system of employee advocacy?

Whether you are a company of 5 or 5,000 people, this book is for you.

Happy reading!

Sarah

PART 1

WHY EMPLOYEE ADVOCACY?

What is employee advocacy?

Put simply, employee advocacy is when the employees of a company are empowered to promote the company they work for.

It mainly concerns using social networks where employees share and promote content via their personal profiles. Content that is either created by the company or is about the company. I say 'mainly concerns' as, of course, we can advocate using our voices and in person, it doesn't have to be via social media. However, when we're talking about 'setting up a system' of employee advocacy, we're talking about using social media, and in most cases, LinkedIn, as the most effective place.

It always surprises me that companies aren't making better use of the voices of their employees to spread the company message. It may be that only 3% of employees share content about their company, but those shares are responsible for driving a 30% increase in the total engagement a company sees. [2]

This happens because, on average, the networks of a company's employees are at least 10 times larger than the company page follower base. And on top of that, when employees share a post, it's seen as three times more authentic. With these figures in mind, it's easy to see that there is tremendous potential in activating employee voices on LinkedIn.

I used to have a social media agency running social media for different types of hospitality clients, mainly pubs. The budgets for each pub were not huge so we had to be resourceful. I came up with the idea to showcase the employees on the pubs' company pages on social media and encourage each employee to then share that content on their personal profiles. We hoped we would get more engagement on the posts, but we got so much more than that!

We saw very quickly that doing this started to generate sales which were directly attributed to the increase in their followers and engagement on social media. The results for many of the pubs were eye-opening. One pub saw an increase in private hire room bookings of over 400%.

76% of people trust content shared by regular employees more than content shared by the company's official channels[3]

What we hadn't anticipated was that doing this also created a healthy and fun 'banter' among the staff. We would offer monthly prizes - usually bottles of alcohol - to the employee whose post got the most engagement. Each month, the pub manager would present the winner with their prize and it became a 'talked about' event. We would post about it on the pub's social media - of course! It was a very low ticket price for the employer to gain a significantly increased brand awareness across their social media channels, and it also created a huge shift in the company culture. The camaraderie among the staff was noticeably different and, what's more, job applications increased almost overnight!

For some pubs, their social media really began to build local community interest. A staff member overheard a parent in the school playground say 'Hey, have you seen the pub's Instagram post today - it's brilliant!' We even got invited to visit the House Of Lords as one of our pubs won 'best social media for a community pub' on the back of our campaign.

In this book, we'll focus on two of the most important benefits of employee advocacy:

1. A happier work environment that leads to lower staff turnover, lower levels of stress among employees, and a better quality workforce
2. Increased sales as a consequence of wider reach, stronger relationships, and stronger positive brand perception

Let's start with the latter.

CHAPTER 1

Increasing the company's sales and profits

From having my own social media agency and teaching social media to pubs and restaurants, to teaching entrepreneurs and businesses all over the world how to use social media and LinkedIn, the one question I hear over and over is this:

"What will be the return on my investment, Sarah?"

It's a reasonable question! Training your workforce costs time and money. Is it worth it?

The answer is a resounding 'yes'! Not only will the company gain more followers and an increase in its brand awareness, but it will also get better quality and more relevant followers.

Chris Boudreaux, author and digital media manager for large companies, was talking about employee advocacy as early as 2013 in his book "The Most Powerful Brand On Earth".

> "We saw that traffic generated by employees converted at around 2.5x the rate of traffic generated by the brand. In fact, employees each generated more than $100,000 worth of sales. In essence, we got more traffic that converted better at a lower cost. Salespeople who regularly share, are 45% more likely to exceed their quotas[4].

Hinge Research Institute found[5] that increased visibility and brand recognition were the top two benefits that firms received from employee advocacy on social media. While visibility and brand recognition can be difficult to measure, making it difficult to prove your return on investment (ROI), Hinge also identified tangible, measurable benefits when implementing an employee advocacy system including:

- Increased inbound web traffic
- Better search engine rankings
- Increased content downloads
- Decreased marketing costs

One concrete finding was that:

> "Nearly 64% of advocates in a formal program credited employee advocacy with attracting and developing new business - and nearly 45% attribute new revenue streams to employee advocacy."

Now we're getting somewhere, right?

Another specific finding in the Hinge study was that social media engagement created a 56% increase in website traffic and a 25.1% increase in revenue! That's powerful! Can a company ignore this?

Take a look at these stats from the study:

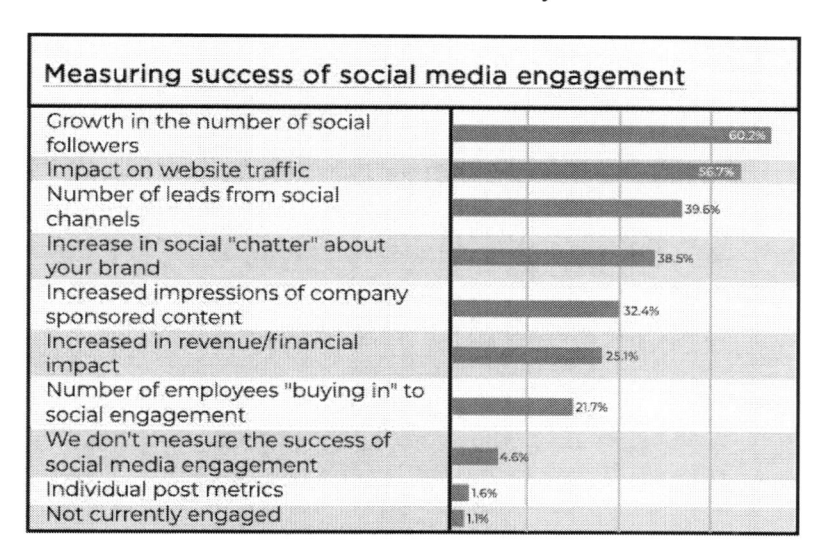

Measuring success of social media engagement	
Growth in the number of social followers	60.2%
Impact on website traffic	56.7%
Number of leads from social channels	39.6%
Increase in social "chatter" about your brand	38.5%
Increased impressions of company sponsored content	32.4%
Increased in revenue/financial impact	25.1%
Number of employees "buying in" to social engagement	21.7%
We don't measure the success of social media engagement	4.6%
Individual post metrics	1.6%
Not currently engaged	1.1%

What's the ROI of an employee advocacy system?

The initial ROI of a system of employee advocacy is measured by looking at the metrics of the personal profiles as well as the company page.

We look at things such as:

1. Number of new followers and connections for each employee
2. Reach and engagement of each post on the company page and personal profiles
3. Number of visitors and followers to the company page

Measuring these metrics in this way helps work out the direction for the page month by month.

As the system evolves, and if a company is using a tracking system, it is possible to track journeys from individuals' posts to the company page or the website. This is invaluable and will help a company hone its content, as well as each employee's activity. It may be worth investing in a platform which supports a system of tracking and recording success.

Tools such as DSMN8 do this; they compared the cost per click of a system of employee advocacy to having a LinkedIn Ads strategy.

According to Lewis Gray, senior marketing manager at DSMN8, the earned media value of LinkedIn ads in 2022 was between $6 and $10 per click - at a very conservative level. DSMN8 announced that the cost of using an employee advocacy system for one of their clients was less than a dollar per click.

> "We're looking at 62 cents a click compared $10 that we've paid in the past on Ads" - Lewis Gray

But the benefits don't stop with increased reach, followers and engagement.

The psychology of why people buy

Jay Baer, bestselling author and market researcher, reported that 92% of consumers trust recommendations from people they know directly. Even anonymous reviewers have a 70% trust rate when they post online about a brand.[6] People trust people - not logos!

> **41% of people believe employees are more trustworthy than CEOs or PR departments**[7]

The reason is that regular employees are often considered, by most of the company's customers, to be on the same level as they are. The psychological balance is more equal. Employees have a lesser stake in the company than the CEO or the marketing department. Therefore, many consumers find it easier to trust what employees say, while feeling that marketing and PR can be 'smoke and mirrors' and may only tell one side of the story. People believe that talking to an employee means they're more likely to get those tricky questions answered with honesty.

So we listen to regular people. Our friends, a neighbour, people we meet at networking events, a colleague, our family. Regular people, with whom we have something in common. People who have experienced the products or services in the way that we are likely to experience them. This is why reviews on Trip Advisor, Amazon and Trust Pilot are so popular - as well as recommendations on LinkedIn!

In fact, approximately two thirds of activities in a buying process have nothing to do with the marketing activities planned by the company. Instead, they have everything to do with people engaging with other people in conversations.[8]

Likewise, many job opportunities are never posted anywhere. They are filled by people already engaged in conversation with current or former employees of the company. The relationships have already been built so it's a smooth transition to the hiring process.

It really is time that companies realise the value of conversations happening between real people, and to embrace not only the fact that they are uncontrollable but that they are a golden opportunity to tap into and should be consistently encouraged and nurtured.

Unfortunately, many companies do not realise the amazing resources they have at their fingertips; resources to begin and continue conversations which lead to sales, better quality hires, and which can help shape the social fabric of the company.

Most companies aren't aware that having a strategy for engaging and empowering their employees from all departments in public conversations has such tremendous potential when it comes to business growth. Instead of relying on one formal, curated voice of a company page, any company, whatever their size or the nature of their business, has the opportunity to initiate and inspire real, human conversations. These are conversations that could help engage and connect employees and people far beyond the reach of the company.

The wasted opportunity on LinkedIn

Seeing LinkedIn as a networking platform rather than a broadcasting tool will enable us to get so much more out of it than just talking about our products or services to a slowly growing and rarely engaged audience. Employee advocacy can be used to find, build and nurture connections with people who were previously strangers by empowering employees to strategically engage in and initiate conversations on LinkedIn. They can warm up audiences and converse in a helpful way that might convert into sales or into one more person willing to share information about the company in places we never considered relevant for promotion - simply because they "know" someone there.

Empowering and teaching employees to use LinkedIn strategically as a networking tool opens up opportunities for them to help spread the company message and grow the company - while simultaneously fostering a culture of belonging, assertiveness and recognition.

Companies spend a huge amount of money honing their brand and sales messages. But are enough people seeing those messages? From where I look, for most companies, the answer is a resounding no! I see too many companies' content on LinkedIn getting such little reach, it's almost a crime.

So how can a company ensure that their content is seen by more people on LinkedIn?

Well...here is something most people don't know:

Posts shared by employees get a 561% higher reach than the same post going out on a company page[9]

Posting the same post on a company page and again on someone's personal profile could dramatically increase the ROI on that post.

Think about the impact of posting something on three personal profiles - or how about 300? The subsequent increase in the reach of that post is potentially vast and certainly bigger than only posting on the company page. Even a company with five employees will see a huge increase in brand awareness of a post on their personal profiles.

Here are just two examples of where we can see how a programme of employee advocacy on LinkedIn has worked:

VISA

Brand Visa launched an employee advocacy programme to shine a light on new and interesting things happening in local markets around the globe, and to position themselves and their employees as thought leaders. Since launching the programme, Visa employees are sharing 6x more than before. Employees sharing content have also influenced 4x more company page followers.

DLA PIPER

DLA Piper, a global law firm, cites that their professionals have influenced 3x as many company page followers and 4x as many company page views after introducing their employee advocacy programme.

10 specific ways employee advocacy can contribute to sales and profits

1. Increased ROI on content production

LinkedIn is structured in such a way that it does not want company pages to monopolise personal content streams. This being the case, the algorithm has been designed to push content from company pages only to a small and highly selected audience. Quite possibly just to other company pages and to 'followers' of the company page who have selected to receive that content in their feeds. The way the LinkedIn algorithm 'places' content makes it very difficult to reach non-following personal profiles with content published only on company pages.

The clickthrough rate of content on personal profiles is double that of company pages. As an example, Thermo Fisher Scientific, after engaging in a system of employee advocacy, had a 62% increase in reach of their company page posts when posted on their employees' personal profiles.

If a post gets a high level of engagement - especially in the first hour or so of it being published - the LinkedIn algorithm will react to that engagement and push the post out to an even wider audience. It makes sense that LinkedIn would want to promote popular and good quality content. Therefore, a brilliant way of increasing the ROI on LinkedIn content is to make employees aware of upcoming posts by key personnel. When, for example, the CEO is going to post thought leadership pieces - if the whole team is notified in advance, they will be prepared to interact with that post when it goes live and thereby create a 'buzz' around that post.

To further increase the reach and engagement of their thought leadership pieces, the CEO should be posting on their personal profile as well as on the company page.

2. Strengthening of the brand message

People are often surprised when I say that it's OK to post the same content on the company page as well as on the personal profiles of the employees. Repeating content is a strategy which can, and should, be utilised. Creating awareness about the company is a process rather than a one-off event.

The LinkedIn feed is bursting with content and, with over a billion personal profiles on LinkedIn, sadly a very small proportion of our audience see our content - even when they are following or are connected to us. Even if someone spent a whole day on LinkedIn, they wouldn't see all the posts of the people they follow.

On top of that, people aren't always fully focused on their computer or phone when they're scrolling through their feeds. From a technical point of view, presenting the same content more than once is a great strategy since it increases the chances of people seeing it.

From an emotional point of view, the 'Marketing Rule of 7' states that a prospect needs to "hear" the advertiser's message at least 7 times before they'll take action to buy that product or service[10].

When you hear a song on the radio that you've heard many times before, it feels nice because you know the lyrics. The familiarity with this song brings feelings of happiness and comfort. You know all the words, and you can sing along. That familiarity creates a feeling of fuzziness and warmth.

A system whereby the same message is posted and staggered over a period of time could increase the impact of that message among its target audience. So by presenting a piece of content on both the company page and employee profiles, perhaps told in slightly different ways, a company is helping its audience feel familiar and comfortable with their brand as well as helping its message become more memorable and remain front of mind for when those customers are ready to buy.

3. Search optimisation

SEO works on LinkedIn in the same way as on the wider internet. Google and LinkedIn are good friends! Certain content and links on LinkedIn will come up in organic search results on Google as well as on LinkedIn.[11]

Employees who are using the correct keywords and phrases on LinkedIn contribute to improved SEO, making it easier for companies and individuals to find the company as they search. This will help the company rank higher in searches on Google, as well as on LinkedIn. Coming up on page one of a Google search is what most companies aspire to. Utilising LinkedIn correctly will increase the chances of this happening.

4. Increased trust in the brand

When employees spend time on LinkedIn offering advice, support and conversation, they are building a perception of kindness and generosity as well as valuable relationships. It seems obvious that, if someone eventually needs or wants what that employee's company has to offer, the first place they go is to the person they know. Employee advocacy turns each employee into a brand ambassador who has the power to influence buying decisions.

A less commonly recognised factor is that, when employees share their experiences, insights and genuine enthusiasm for the company, it creates an authentic connection with the brand. Something subconscious happens here. Positive messages about the company, its ethos, its products or services, help the audience more closely relate to and develop trust in the brand, which is likely to bring in more business and at a higher price.

5. Increased outbound sales

One of the main differences between personal profiles and company pages on LinkedIn is that it's only possible to outreach from personal profiles. It is not possible to search for and approach potential customers from a company page. This makes perfect sense, knowing people want to talk to people, not to companies.

When employees start to use LinkedIn for proactive outreach, the return on their investment of time can be enormous. Unlike any other platform, it is possible to be extremely targeted when outreaching on LinkedIn - something which is a surprise to many sales teams I work with.

6. Increased referrals

A study from the Wharton School of Business shows that referred customers have a 16% higher lifetime value than average customers.[12] This means that over time, customers who come via a referral will bring more revenue to a business than those acquired elsewhere.

In contrast to affiliate marketing which is based on commission payments or rewards, the referrals I'm talking about here - 'word of mouth marketing' - do not involve payment in any form. When employees begin talking about their company in a positive way, what happens is different, and potentially more powerful, because it's based on genuine interest in the company's well-being. If we know someone is benefiting financially from a recommendation, the level of trust drops, and the recommendation loses its authenticity. Employee advocacy has a much different flavour, meaning conversion on those referrals is higher and, as I've mentioned, so is the lifetime value.

7. Lower customer acquisition costs

New customer acquisition is time-consuming and expensive. A company's employee advocacy strategy should include ambitions to retain their existing customers as well as acquire new ones.

By regularly appearing in previous and current customers' feeds, a company's employees and the company message can stay top of mind for when those customers are ready to buy again. It's not even necessary to 'add value' the whole time. These customers already know the quality of the goods and service they received when working with the company. It really is simply about providing a constant reminder of who you are.

An occasional DM or comment on customers' and partners' posts can really help solidify a relationship between a previous customer and an employee, and therefore the company. Using employees to keep in touch with previous and current customers can reduce new customer acquisition costs while also leading to new sales. One of the best ways of staying in touch is to generously support their content with a targeted commenting strategy. LinkedIn doesn't put a limit on how many times we can comment on other people's posts!

8. Increased quality and fit of new hires

Employee advocacy can lead to a 20% increase in job applicants and a 50% reduction in cost-per-hire.

> **Companies that integrate advocacy programmes into their marketing strategies see an average of 26% increase in year-on-year revenue**[13]

LinkedIn comes in second, after Indeed, as the most popular tool used when looking for a new job (LinkedIn 57%, Indeed 62%). Each week over 61 million people are actively looking through LinkedIn for their next position[14] and eight people are hired every minute on the platform. With statistics like these, why would a company NOT use LinkedIn to its fullest capacity to showcase itself and attract the best quality candidates?

With a dedicated job search page housing a multitude of filters, it is possible for job seekers to find their next position without the need for a recruiter. That in itself is a cost saver worth exploring, putting more emphasis on candidates who are searching for career opportunities rather than on job advertising.

People also use LinkedIn to keep an eye on specific companies they may be considering when they're thinking about career progression. It is estimated that 51% of job seekers are passive candidates[15]- they are thinking about getting a new job but they haven't started actively searching yet. These people are constantly paying attention and gathering information, and it's all happening on LinkedIn. They're following companies, reading articles, joining events, and engaging in conversations.

If a company can capture their attention, there are potential opportunities for hiring someone before they even start looking and interacting with other companies. This potentially could not only attract a higher quality candidate but also save the company a fortune in recruitment and agency fees.

TRUE STORY

A company I had been working with for a while came to me with a specific problem - they couldn't hire a new team member. They had paid out a fortune to recruiters but the candidates they were being offered were far from the quality they needed.

We had already created a series of posts focused on personalising the brand so we decided to focus more heavily on content like this which humanised the company, shone a light on the staff, and talked about what was going on 'behind the scenes'. The thinking was that, once they showed the genuinely happy and cohesive office environment on their company page, that would attract applicants who valued that in their job and were therefore more likely to fit in. We then created some specific 'we are hiring' posts, highlighting the positive aspects of working with the company and talking about tangible benefits such as finishing early on a Friday, many training opportunities, chances for promotion etc.

We also created posts about the less tangible aspects of working at the company. We talked about how Jon made an awesome cuppa, that birthdays were a big celebration and how everyone supported each other and enjoyed being together. These more personalised posts were the ones which made the difference. A different calibre of applications started to come in. A successful candidate was chosen. The cost to the company was a tenth of the cost of a recruiter's commission, and the new hire assimilated into the company really quickly and easily as they were already aligned with the company culture.

By talking about the company culture on the company page, and by using the employees to engage in conversations on LinkedIn using their personal profiles, potential hires will be able to easily monitor and get an understanding of the company culture. Showcasing a positive, inclusive, diverse and open-minded culture will go a long way to attracting a high calibre of applicants for jobs when they arise.

Employees can also be used more directly to promote the company and partake in spreading the word about vacancies using their network of growing connections. Word-of-mouth is powerful!

9. Increased employee retention

Hiring a new employee is not a cheap or easy process. Onboarding new staff is expensive in terms of time and money.

> - For high-turnover, low-paying jobs, companies can expect to pay around 16% of the employee's salary to replace them
> - For mid-range positions, this figure goes up to around 20%
> - Replacing executive positions, companies can expect to pay up to 213% of a salary[16]

Employees taking part in an employee advocacy system will often develop a more trusting relationship with the company, which can go a long way to help that employee to feel a valued part of the company. This is likely to add to job satisfaction, leading to them staying in the job longer.

10. Network of external brand ambassadors

If by now you haven't realised the power of using LinkedIn to create a network of brand ambassadors, this next piece may do the trick and change the way you use the LinkedIn platform!

LinkedIn is made up of 1st, 2nd and 3rd+ degree connections. When you connect with someone, every single one of their connections becomes yours too! So if you connect with someone who has 14,000 1st degree connections, you immediately acquire 14,000 2nd degree connections.

So what?, you might think.

What happens when someone becomes a 'friend of a friend' in real life? They move one step closer to being a friend of yours. Because of the mutual connection, a level of trust begins to develop. LinkedIn works in exactly the same way.

In fact, you can leverage the connection and invite those 2nd degree connections to become 1st degree connections. When there is a mutual connection, it's not hard to build on the relationship.

Employees consistently using LinkedIn as a networking tool will grow their networks in a genuine and relevant way. Their activity will help create a loyal fan base of potential brand ambassadors. Some of these people will engage with all or many of the employee posts and/or the posts on company pages. This has the potential to bring eyes over to the company page. Someone who was previously a stranger to the company has now become a brand ambassador.

CHAPTER 2

Building a happier company culture

Hopefully now you are aware of how an employee advocacy strategy could potentially increase sales and profits for a company, although you may not have a clue where to start (don't worry, I cover this later in the book).

It is far less common that managers are aware of the positive cultural implications. When I discuss employee advocacy with business owners they are fascinated by the concept of using the system to help level up company culture. Let's start with a practical example.

Providing online training, company X doubled in size during the pandemic when people wanted to upskill but couldn't do this in person. To meet demand, the company had hired staff really quickly and from wherever they could find skilled trainers.

The CEO confided in me, saying he was saddened that he hadn't met half of his workforce as they lived all over the world. It was too difficult and expensive to get everyone together in person and the team therefore met online regularly for meetings (along with the rest of the world at that time).

A big problem with online meetings is that the attendees don't do 'small talk'. Meeting online is fairly hard work and if you have more than four people on a video call, it's difficult for conversation to flow naturally. The consequence for this company was that nobody really knew their colleagues, the manager didn't really know the employees, and their company culture had not had a chance to form in any intended way.

I suggested a different approach that would suit virtual staff much better and would potentially provide team benefits they couldn't even have achieved when they were a smaller team all working in the same location. I explained; employee advocacy is about developing and strengthening the culture through increased employee engagement, visibility and celebration of good work, and that this can be achieved through increased LinkedIn activity.

The business owner's eyes lit up, seeing this as a potential solution to the disconnect he saw within his team. He immediately understood that, by using LinkedIn more deliberately, his teams could find a place to communicate together in a non-threatening and easy way, strengthening the sense of belonging and loyalty in the company.

According to LinkedIn's official report on employee advocacy, employees at socially engaged companies are 27% more likely to feel optimistic about their company's future, and 15% more likely to feel connected to co-workers beyond their core teams

Following each other on LinkedIn and engaging with each other's content is a great way to create a sense of optimism about their future at the company.

According to Dr Robert Waldinger[17], one of the key factors that helps workers be happier and healthier at work is how connected they feel with their colleagues. I don't think many people fully appreciate how valuable a happy working environment is to most employees.

We know that those who have friends at work are happier, which obviously has many positive effects on the company as a whole. When we know our colleagues well, we become more helpful, more considerate of other peoples' feelings and well-being, and more aware of their unique talents. We become better collaborators and promoters of a positive and attractive company culture.

What is company culture and how does it become an effective business instrument?

There is a famous saying by Richard Branson - "Create the kind of workplace and company culture that will attract great talent. Then, if you hire brilliant people, they will make work feel more like play."

Simply put, work culture is the 'rules of behaviour' in a workplace. It's how employees treat each other. It's how managers issue instructions, how employees interact and collaborate to get the job done. It's the expectations of the employees on how to behave and their perception of what is important. It's how a work environment 'feels'. It's the company's DNA.

A positive work culture isn't just about table tennis tables and bonuses; it's about creating a genuinely happy place where people want to come to work and be productive. It should be a safe space that inspires personal growth and active kindness, and an environment that facilitates contribution to company growth. "It's a living and breathing thing that's evolving all the time," said J.C. Herrera, Chief Human Resources Officer at cybersecurity firm CrowdStrike.

A study from Forbes recently revealed that happy employees are as much as 20% more productive in the workplace than unhappy employees.[18] It's clear that the success of a company is inextricably linked to the happiness of its employees. Happy employees are also less stressed. It's no secret that stress has many negative impacts on employees and the workplace as a whole[19].

For many employees, LinkedIn is their favourite place to share work-related information and experiences. You will see posts about the pride and the joy employees receive from being a part of a supportive and genuine community at work. People don't want to just 'go to work' anymore. They want to have a sense of pride in what they do and in what the company produces. Employees want to feel a sense of belonging in their workplace and they are often a lot more willing to contribute to that than many employers imagine. In fact, allowing them to do so is a key denominator to encourage them to stay loyal to the company.

I need to address a misguided assumption that keeps some managers from engaging in employee advocacy. They worry about the additional workload put upon already stressed employees. It might help to know that 77% of employees are already active on their own social media while at work.[20] Implementing an employee advocacy system may be about redirecting this energy to creating a larger, positive effect for the company and, as you'll see, for the employees too.

Employers have a responsibility to help manage and prevent stress at work. Managing workload and allowing autonomy are a part of that. Encouraging employees to communicate with each other on LinkedIn can actually provide the very feeling of teamwork and belonging that has been missing in the organisation. Employee advocacy can be a significant lever for employee happiness and productive conversations internally as well as externally. It's a lot healthier for the employee when a company encourages, rather than tries to silence, conversation.

The benefits of a stronger work culture are extensive. Companies with a strong positive culture outperform their competition. According to Culture.io[21], when compared to the bottom quartile of engagement, companies in the top quartile of financial performance can boast:

> - 17% higher productivity rates
> - 21% higher profitability
> - 20% higher sales

The same study found that:

> - over a third of US workers are willing to turn down the perfect job if company culture isn't a good fit
> - 68% see benefits and corporate culture as more important than their salary

All in all, there is good reason to consider new strategies to cultivate and promote an engaging company culture. I'm not suggesting that getting employees using LinkedIn will immediately solve all staff issues within the company, but it can contribute towards having a more connected workforce.

8 ways to use employee advocacy to create a happier company culture

1. Upskilling employees

When I train organisations, I often see that providing opportunities for employees to upskill uncovers talents which they didn't know they had.

According to a study by Willis Towers Watson, 70% of "high-retention-risk" employees want to leave because they see no future advancement in the current job"[22].

This is further emphasised in a study[23] by Robert Half, which revealed that a strong learning culture leads to a 30–50% higher retention rate in companies:

> *"Upskilling staff is a great way to show your employees that you care about their progression and help them feel there's something 'in it for them', which can in turn boost employee morale and improve job satisfaction among your teams."*

It would be a short-sighted company that didn't want to improve their employees' knowledge and skills - particularly in times of constant technological advancement. Taking people away from their desks and putting them in a room together to learn something new can be turned into a fun activity, leaving employees feeling happier, more connected to each other and highly valued!

Copywriting and design are just two skills used in running a personal LinkedIn profile. It's highly possible that someone in the company realises they have a skill for creating images on Canva, or they re-discover their love of humour or writing when they start creating posts.

If a company doesn't have its own design team or internal marketing department, a current employee may 'shine' enough to be given a new role in the company! Discovering new talents is empowering and it's possible that employees could use their new-found skills in their position at work.

2. Sharing personal information

Learning more about our colleagues and the people we work with is an instrumental part of workplace culture and provides a number of benefits for the organisation. Teams that know each other have better relationships, understand each other and play to one another's strengths.

This isn't just hearsay, it's fact:[24]

1. 70% of workers say having friends at work is crucial to a happy working life
2. 58% of men and 74% of women said they would refuse a promotion for a higher paying job if it meant they wouldn't get along with their colleagues
3. 50% of people with a best friend at work reported that they feel a strong connection with their company, meaning they are less likely to leave and more inclined to advocate for the company

Having more depth of information about our colleagues enables relationships to build more deeply at work. This can potentially create a genuinely happier and more productive company culture.

3. Recognition of good work

Many companies are guilty of not giving enough praise for good work and results. Publicly acknowledging employees for outstanding performance and making them feel appreciated is likely to lead to increased motivation, higher performance and a greater loyalty to the company.

Congratulating an employee in a LinkedIn post is a perfect way of showcasing someone's work and making them feel good about their efforts. Encouraging other team members to comment on, and share such a post will involve the whole workforce in the praise. This will help bring people together as well as potentially inspire some of the other staff to want to achieve and receive recognition in the same way. Thus this small act of gratitude holds the potential to promote an atmosphere of community and working towards the common goal, while also increasing productivity.

When employees proactively demonstrate appreciation, affirmation and respect for their colleagues, they can foster better team performance as a whole. [25]

Celebrating 'wins' is not only good for the 'winner' and their colleagues but it also promotes the company to its audience.

Congratulating an employee for winning an award, smashing their targets or taking part in a charity event is the type of content that people find easy to comment on, demonstrating their team spirit and appreciative skills. Apart from the genuine desire to congratulate, most are aware how celebrating achievements of others also sheds a positive light on their own personal brand. Therefore this type of post is an effective wheel to generate engagement and promote the company as a winning place to be to a larger audience.

4. Including remote workers and freelancers

We're all aware of the advantages of working remotely. However, it does have its downfalls, one of which is that it is harder to disseminate knowledge about the company when teams don't have the opportunity for casual chit-chat. Generating conversations about the organisation, about its successes, about its clients, about its work processes, even about new products and new services is more difficult.

When people are all in the same office working together, they overhear conversations and they sometimes find themselves taking part in those conversations. This doesn't happen if they're working remotely. Sending out countless emails, company updates here, company changes there, new policies, new ideas, new products etc, rarely helps - as everyone knows it's not really an invitation to have a conversation. Furthermore, the company often limits this type of communication to its directly employed staff and doesn't fully embrace freelancers or others who might feel they are a part of the workforce.

It's important that all staff, whether directly employed or not, feel a part of what's happening within the company. This could mean feeling that they're up to date with what's happening in terms of new products and services, new members of staff, new clients, thoughts and ideas. All this information can be shared in a professional way on the company page for the benefit of those outside the company, but also for members of the team without the need for lengthy emails, memos etc.

Having discourse on the company page should be encouraged. Such discourse should be professional at all times, never forgetting that LinkedIn is a public platform. Laying the information out for all to see can only help bring cohesion and increase values of loyalty and a feeling of belonging amongst the staff.

5. Celebrating personal milestones

As well as hard work and results, it's important to celebrate other things too. Wishing someone a happy birthday or congratulating them on an anniversary in a post on LinkedIn is likely to foster a feeling of well-being and harmony within the community of the company. Communicating publicly in this way has the added advantage of projecting positive messaging for the public to see, which shows a company cares about its employees.

Research from the Harvard Business Review shows that birthdays are one of the three main days when an unhappy employee is likely to hand in their notice. This is because it's a time when people traditionally take stock of their life and realise another year has passed and, if they're dissatisfied, they are more likely to take action there and then.

The same study revealed that people's job searching activities increase by 12% just before their birthday.[26]

It is equally important to recognise longevity. Even if the employee doesn't have an active LinkedIn profile, congratulating long service in a LinkedIn post is an easy way for them to feel involved in the LinkedIn strategy and the company as a whole.

Any form of recognition from a senior member of staff helps employees see that their company values them as well as valuing their contributions to the success of their team and the company overall. This is particularly key when organisations grow or change. It helps employees build a sense of security in their value to the company, motivating them to continue their dedication and hard work.

6. Giving each employee a 'voice'

Creating an environment for people to feel confident to speak up has huge positive results for each employee as well as for the workforce as a whole. Employees who are not comfortable 'broadcasters' may be frightened of making mistakes. They're less likely to communicate their ideas to their peers as well as to try new things and push themselves.

Apart from contributing strongly to building their personal brands, being allowed and even invited to have their own voice creates confidence which is a tremendous asset to the company. Having a voice in the company will give each employee a sense of agency over their company's future as well as over their future in the company.

Confident employees are more likely to be engaged than intimidated by the challenges their work presents, and they may be willing to step outside their comfort zones, make necessary decisions, and put forward bold ideas. As such, confident employees are likely to grow into good leaders. As they use their voices on LinkedIn, all of the above mentioned benefits have the potential to come into play.

7. Creating a culture of autonomy

When employees take ownership of their work, they are likely to treat the business they are working for — and its money — more as if it were their own. They are likely to make decisions thoughtfully, responsibly, and with more care. Employees who feel they have autonomy are likely to be more driven, motivated, and have more initiative. Employees who feel they can make their own decisions are more likely to seek creative and innovative ways to improve and develop what they are doing, rather than going through the motions and fulfilling the minimum required, or worse still, stagnating. In short, a company with employees who take ownership is a company that's moving forward. It also creates a much more positive and fulfilling working environment for everyone.

Giving teams autonomy and ownership requires trust. Millennials surveyed are 22 times more likely to seek out work in companies with a culture that prioritises a trusting environment.[27] When employees feel their superiors are breathing down their necks, it can make them feel stifled and compromised. They feel like a cog in someone else's wheel.

Giving someone ownership of their content, their comments and who they connect with on LinkedIn, will foster an environment of confidence; that they are trusted to do this on their own. This is likely to bring feelings of trust and give an unspoken permission for employees to flourish.

8. Onboarding new employees

Onboarding a new employee can be a lengthy and expensive process. The challenges of this can be exacerbated if the position is remote. A successful employee engagement strategy can help a new hire get to know their colleagues before they've even signed the contract! By the time their start date comes, they will feel like they already know everyone as they've been following their posts. This will give the new hire the knowledge they need to feel confident and secure in their new environment.

Encouraging a new hire to comment on posts and introduce themselves to their fellow team members on LinkedIn will help them feel part of the team and will help the existing employees get to know their new colleague. On joining the company, a post on the page introducing them to the team will enable everyone to add their comments and welcome their new team member to the company.

This will create an easy platform for the new colleague to reply to comments and begin building relationships with their new colleagues.

CHAPTER 3

Promoting thought leadership among the employees

For an employee advocacy system to work effectively, each employee needs to understand the benefits to themselves over and above potential fiscal growth of the company. There will be employees who understand that their actions can drive more profit to the company and this will be enough for them to invest their time in the programme. In this chapter, I would like to open your eyes to the vast benefits that an employee advocacy system can have for each employee.

One of the biggest individual opportunities for the employee is to get their employer's support to step into a role of thought leadership in public. Some specialists feel that overly promoting themselves might be frowned upon by their employer and create a sense of them not being happy, or being about to leave the company. These people might have chosen to keep their head down out of fear of losing career opportunities in the company.

Thought leadership is something that can apply to people at all levels of the company. The CEO, the tech teams, HR and marketing all have their levels of expertise in their own respective fields.

Establishing oneself as a thought leader is for those who can, and want, to make a positive contribution to their careers and the company as a whole by publishing their thoughts and research in public. A system of employee advocacy is the ideal vehicle for this. Having the support of one's colleagues and bosses gives a head start to someone publishing content on LinkedIn. This can be crucial when someone is starting out.

Benefits for the employee

1. Building and leveraging a personal brand

When someone is using LinkedIn to display their high level of knowledge, as well as their ability to collate and present that knowledge in a coherent, relevant and interesting way, other experts in the same field will want to associate with them.

People are aware that associating with a thought leader can help increase their audience and credibility. When actively participating in industry conversations, sharing thought-provoking insights, and offering solutions to industry challenges, whether they're CEOs or other team members, opportunities can arise. These could be invitations to be guests on podcasts or at conferences, interviews, guest writing, and even publishing and book deals.

The impact of this can be huge in terms of profile building and extra income as well as positioning for the individual and, of course, the company.

2. Establishing credibility

The more good quality content someone produces and the more value they add to people's professional lives, the higher their credibility and integrity will be. Reading one or two interesting thoughts from someone about their respective level of expertise is a good start but, once someone begins publishing regularly on LinkedIn, their audience will start to seek them out as a trusted voice and a person to pay attention to and listen to.

If someone is consistently demonstrating their knowledge in a specific niche, with content and comments on LinkedIn, they are validating their name as a trusted expert in their area of work

Their standing in the industry will become firmly established and their name will be on everyone's lips as an authoritative figure, which they can continue to validate as they build their engagement and audience. This isn't going to happen overnight; credibility and integrity take time to earn, but it definitely works on LinkedIn.

3. Community Building

When someone begins to drive engagement and interest among their target audience, they will notice that they are building a community around them where people come together to discuss ideas and learn from their insights; their content becomes a valuable source of information and inspiration. As a result, their followers will want to share their content and talk about it, both on their own feeds and when commenting on other people's posts. This will bring about an exponential growth, so the community will start pulling in new audiences, sharing the thought leader's content with even more people.

4. To better understand customer needs

When the posts start receiving comments, those comments can be used to find out more about what the audience wants and what they're thinking. This, in turn, will help the content creator tailor their content accordingly to ensure it taps directly into what will resonate deeply with their audience. By using open language, and directly asking people their thoughts, it's possible for a company to elicit quite detailed information about their customers which they can use in all kinds of scenarios.

5. Positioning with other thought leaders

Demonstrating thought leadership in a certain industry can help someone build relationships with other thought leaders. By interacting with 'influencers' in their industry, CEOs and employees will not only open themselves up to collaborations with other thought leaders but they will be positioning themselves as an original thinker and innovator.

6. Opportunities for career advancement

For an employee, having an active presence on LinkedIn won't go unnoticed by their colleagues and bosses. Most of our activity on LinkedIn is widely visible for all the public to see. This means that, as someone builds their audience and influence across the platform (and therefore across the world!), they become a more valuable asset to their organisation. The benefits of this internally can be extremely powerful in terms of salary and career progression.

7. Personal growth

Engaging in employee advocacy requires individuals to stay updated on industry trends and adapt to changes. An employee who wants to share knowledge needs to accrue that knowledge through their own work, experimenting with new ideas and also by researching others' work.

Engaging with others on LinkedIn will help employees gain significant knowledge about the market, the competition, new technologies, and many other issues within the industry. This commitment to continuous learning and growth contributes to an individual's personal brand as someone who is forward-thinking and stays relevant in their field.

In summary, employee advocacy empowers individuals to take control of their personal brand and enable them to have agency.

PART 2

LAYING THE FOUNDATIONS

A successful system of employee advocacy needs to be really well thought out before it's begun. One of the goals is to drive traffic to the company page. This means it is essential that the page is fully optimised and is regularly presenting high value, interesting content which is relevant to its desired audience.

I see a movement beginning where LinkedIn company pages are visited more times than websites. A company page must therefore operate like a mini website; a place where potential customers can find out more about the products and services of the company. But a company page should do more. A good company page also shows the human side of the company, highlighting the ethos and beliefs and, of course, the staff of the company. Company pages are relatively easy to update without the need for a web developer or technical team.

Setting up the page for maximum appeal is crucial. Clients I work with usually experience an increase in enquiries within weeks after we redesign the company page, making it more search engine optimised and on brand. Congruent with the website, a good company page tells the company's story and clearly states what the company does for its clients, how it works and where it is based.

For a recent client, less than a week after making changes to an already completed page, two enquiries had come in via the page, and later converted into sales with a value of over £12,000. Imagine the ROI this company will get as we start expanding their reach and visibility!

If you do nothing else, update your company page!

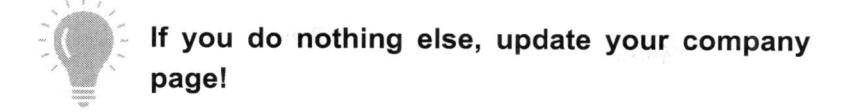

There has been a huge cultural shift in recent years to use LinkedIn as the first place to find out about a potential employee or someone we meet at a networking event. When meeting someone in a professional context, the first place we go in order to find out more about them or to continue the relationship, is their LinkedIn personal profile. After visiting someone's personal profile to connect, the next obvious step is to click through to their company page - a journey that is so much easier than having to navigate to the company website.

It's time for companies to be prepared for this and realise the wasted opportunity if they don't optimise the company page. LinkedIn is investing more and more into company pages, and it's time for companies to do the same.

CHAPTER 4

Creating and growing a powerful company page

Like any system, the roots need to be firmly established for it to flourish. Before any employee advocacy system is started, the first two steps are to have a fully optimised company page and a content strategy.

The company page will form the 'hub' of everyone's activity and will shape the level of activity of each of the participants. The whole system of employee advocacy will spring from, and return to, the company page. The system cannot operate without a strong and powerful company page which regularly produces high quality content.

LinkedIn rewards best practice, and filling in all the information on the company page is considered best practice. Whether or not a company decides to implement a system of employee advocacy, having a fully completed and active company page leads to a much better brand perception and potentially a huge shift in brand awareness and customer growth:

> Company pages with complete information get 30% more weekly views.[28]
> Companies with fully optimised company pages and which are active on their pages see a 7x increase in average impressions per follower and an 11x increase in clicks per follower. That's how happy LinkedIn is with your decision to show up professionally on the platform.

Apart from filling in all the sections, the appearance and content on a LinkedIn company page needs to be appealing to its target audience. It is acceptable to copy and paste sections of your website onto a company page. Congruence is important. Don't leave those visitors confused or disappointed. If they've bothered to come to your company page, give that captive audience something they will recognise if they already know the brand and also ensure they're entertained and informed when they get there.

Admin status

Admins are those who have access to the page and can make changes. There are different levels of admin roles which give access to different features and also a different entry point to the account.

Many people don't see the significance of the different admin roles and I have seen many companies get tripped up by this. If only one employee has all the admin rights and they leave or they're sick, no current employee can log into the page to make changes or add content or even add further admins!

1. Super admin

Super admin status is the highest level of admin. Super admins can do anything on the page including adding and removing any type of admin, editing page information, and deactivating the page. Their main landing page when they log in is the super admin view.

The creator of the page automatically has super admin status. My advice is to have at least two super admins. One should be the CEO or person least likely to leave the company. It's essential you have a super admin who can take control of the page at any time if, for example, the other super admin is ill or leaves the company.

2. Content admin

The next level down, content admin has permission to create and manage page content, including posts (as well as boosting posts), events and jobs. Their main landing page is the content admin view. They can also view and record page metrics, post jobs, boost or manage organic posts, create events and more.

3. Curator

A person with curator status has permission to view and export page analytics and create content. This includes the ability to recommend content on the My Company tab if they're also an employee. They cannot create or post content of their own.

4. Analyst

A person with analyst status only has permission to monitor the page's performance through analytics. Analysts have limited access to the page in third-party tools. They will only have access to the Analytics tab of a page, which is also their main landing page.

5. Paid media admin

In order to create and run ads, a page will need a paid media admin or admins. There are three different levels of paid media admin. I won't go further into this here since this book is not about LinkedIn ads.

Seven Strategies to grow a company page

Have you ever picked blackberries? Those tiny dark purple fruits which grow wild in many parts of the world and are waiting for you to pick them, take them home and use them for wonderful pies and jams! Picking the first blackberry, or bramble, is exciting - but seeing it on its own in the big tub makes the task of getting enough berries for baking a pie seem a bit daunting. Keep picking those blackberries - one, two, three at a time - and soon you see the tub filled with enough of the delicious fruit that you're thinking of starting a jam factory!

Adopt that mindset to growing your company page and you will succeed.

I give you this small encouragement because growing a company page is significantly harder than growing a personal profile, which is why we need a different system to grow it. The system of employee advocacy is really important for the visibility of an organisation. We need to amplify our efforts with the power of the employees.

Of course there are various strategies which can be employed to help grow the page. And when I say grow the page, what I mean is to bring more people to see the content on it. It takes time to grow a page following but with consistency and tenacity it will happen!

At the time of writing, the average organic reach rate for LinkedIn company pages is just 3.03%.[29] The real power of getting people to follow a page is that a follower, if they have their notifications switched on, will get notified by LinkedIn whenever content is posted on the page. Therefore, there is a much higher likelihood that the follower will see the content published as they can go straight to it from the notification without having to scroll endlessly through their feed. This is a golden opportunity for people to be directed to take action, head to the page and read the content!

For a new page owner, it's good to know that, according to LinkedIn, once pages gain 150 followers, their opportunity for growth becomes exponential. So, what are these strategies to get to, and (far) beyond, the magic 150 followers?

1. Invite connections to follow the page

Super admins can invite up to 100 of their personal connections each month to follow the company page.

Actually, that's not quite right - some company page admins are blessed with being able to invite 250 connections a month. LinkedIn awards these extra connections fairly randomly but it seems LinkedIn favours pages which are 'active'.

If, on the first of every month, each super admin makes it a priority to capitalise on these numbers and invite as many of their personal connections as possible, the followers will noticeably increase. This is another reason why it's important for any super admins on the company page to increase the number of connections on their personal profile, alongside growing the company page.

As it's possible to have up to 50 super admins on a page, you may be thinking that it would be useful to assign everyone as a super admin. Not advised! Super admins have a great deal of 'power' on the page, even the power to shut the entire page down, so it is advisable to give out this status with caution!

As an extra bonus, each time someone accepts a request to follow the page, a new credit is given to invite another connection. This highlights the importance of choosing your invitees with care and pick those that are most likely to accept the invitation to follow.

2. Share the company page link

Add a link to your company page on your website, in email footers of all relevant employees and in all marketing materials. Adding a call to action will encourage people to click the link. You can use phrases such as 'find out more' or simply 'visit our LinkedIn page'.

3. Check the 'activity tab' daily

The activity tab is where any notifications show up. If a company page has been mentioned in a post, or if someone has commented on a post published on the page, it will show as a notification in the activity tab. A good admin should take action and respond as quickly as possible to all comments. Leaving unanswered comments on posts does not look good for the company and it's also a wasted opportunity to engage with a person who so clearly showed their interest. Positive comments should be appreciated and negative comments need to be tackled instantly in order to protect the company brand.

4. Publish amazing content on a consistent basis

When someone has arrived at the company page, it's important that there's something for them to see and also a reason for them to stay. Bear in mind that company pages posting on LinkedIn daily will see a 2x higher engagement rate than those that don't. Company pages are structured in a very organised fashion, with a row of tabs across the top. Clicking the 'posts' tab to see all the content ever published on the page is a simple one-click.

5. Promote events via your page

LinkedIn events can be run via both personal profiles and company pages. When I say LinkedIn events, I don't necessarily mean events happening on LinkedIn. LinkedIn has a system whereby it's possible to publicise an event which is being hosted on or off LinkedIn. Using the events tab on the company page as a vehicle to inform and invite your audience to your event, whether it's online or in person, is a simple and powerful strategy and should be investigated.

6. Hosting LinkedIn 'lives' from your page

Video gets 5x more engagement on LinkedIn than written content, and live video gets 24x more.[30] LinkedIn lives are a fantastic way to appeal to and grow a LinkedIn audience, and it's now possible to host live and audio events on LinkedIn via your company page.

Live events sit under the 'video' tab on your company page for all to see, so visitors to a page can easily sort through and find valuable content.

Lives could be in the form of interviews with clients or influencers. Inviting guests on live events - video or audio - puts the company in front of their guests' audiences too, so it's worth adopting a targeted approach to invitees and the topics of conversation.

It's also a good strategy to use lives to add value to audiences and simultaneously promote the business. Talking about the products and services of the company, and the problems they solve, will further engage audiences and encourage them to buy. More on this in Chapter 5: Content strategy for a company page.

7. Creating a branded hashtag

Creating a branded hashtag is a clever way of increasing the chances of a brand name being remembered. Use it often as part of a marketing and branding strategy and it will become part of the brand. It's like a company having their own slogan or strapline. Some examples are:

- 'Just do it' - makes you feel like running, no?
- 'Because you're worth it' - don't know about you but I just want to swoosh my hair at this point!
- 'Every Little Helps' (that's a UK reference, sorry!)

These all are reminders of the brands they represent and are extremely powerful brand awareness tools.

There is a process for registering your own hashtag, however, it's lengthy and expensive. It would be far simpler for a company to create and repeat a hashtag over and over again. The plan being that the hashtag will become synonymous with that company. It would be short-sighted for anyone else to use it.

For example, my branded hashtag is 'LinkedInSimplified'. I haven't seen anyone else use it and I can only hope that nobody ever will. I even incorporate it into a sentence which I use regularly: 'Just keeping #LinkedInSimplified for CEO's, corporates and teams.' If people see the hashtag enough times, they will think of me each time they see it and remember that I like to keep #LinkedInSimplified. It would be an unwise branding exercise for another company to try to adopt someone else's hashtag.

A branded hashtag is used as a status symbol and a way of recognising and remembering a company, so it's important that it is used regularly and consistently.

Repeated use of relevant keywords can help a company come up higher in LinkedIn searches as well as on Google. This can be achieved by repeatedly using a hashtag which is relevant to a company's industry and may be used as a search phrase by others.

CHAPTER 5

Content strategy for the company page

No system of employee advocacy can work unless there is good quality content for employees to advocate! Creating content which they look forward to posting and feel they can really engage with is the key here. Dry, dull content will not inspire employees to act and will not encourage them to create content for posting on their personal profiles.

Before engaging employees in sharing and interacting with company page content, it's necessary to have a company page content strategy that:

1. Appeals to the extended audience of the company
2. Employees will be proud to post on their personal profiles

3. Is varied enough to appeal to the different company departments
4. Presents a rounded picture of the company; its values and ethos as well as its products or services

1. Who is the company creating content for?

Having a clear vision of who it is that the company is talking to and wants to attract is the fundamental starting block when creating a content strategy.

LinkedIn is a place where people talk to each other and share information with their wider network. A powerful content strategy will seek to leverage different groups of people in order to spread the reach of the company message.

This means that a company needs different types of content to appeal to their different audiences:

> **Potential customers**
> When a company speaks to their ideal customers via their content, it will bring potential customers closer. By identifying customers' needs, problems and struggles in their content, a company demonstrates that they fully understand the needs of their audience and can help them.

> **Current or previous customers**
> Sharing customers' success stories in their content can help bring new customers, as well as appeal to current customers. Humans are social beings and it

matters to us when someone we know had a good experience with a product or a company.

Tagging customers in relevant posts can also bring those customers over to the page. As most of our LinkedIn activity is transparent, it's likely that comments someone makes on a company's posts will get seen by some of their connections and followers - in turn bringing them to the page too.

Engaging and reconnecting with previous and current customers before tagging them in a post can lead directly to repeat sales!

> **Suppliers**

The audiences of a company's suppliers are likely to overlap with those of the company. By talking about their suppliers in their content, a company has the potential to appeal to a wider and relevant audience. It is worth bearing in mind that the success of a supplier will increase alongside that of its customer, so they have a vested interest in helping that company's page get more reach. What supplier wouldn't get a little adrenalin hit when they see their name tagged in a post from one of their customers? If they're running their LinkedIn strategy, they know it's valuable for them to hop over, comment on that post or even 'share' it, thus increasing brand awareness for all concerned.

> **Influencers and other thought leaders**

The concept of being an influencer in the traditional sense of the word never took off on LinkedIn in the same way as it did on Instagram, but this doesn't mean to say that influencers don't exist here. Anyone who can influence decision making and purchasing decisions is an influencer. Identifying who the relevant influencers are, and creating content that inspires them to engage with it, drives brand awareness and even direct sales to the company.

> **Referral partners**
> Using partners to help promote each other's business is a strategy many companies employ. If a company can create a symbiotic relationship with another company which is relevant in the industry, and talk about each other in posts, brand awareness for both companies can grow much faster.
>
> Advocacy doesn't have to be just for employees, it can be for partners and customers too. The social media scheduling and advocacy tool Agorapulse has implemented a system of ambassador advocacy where a collection of customer ambassadors are encouraged to share the content from the Agorapulse social media pages onto their own social media profiles. The system is, of course, monitored using Agorapulse's own ambassador platform.

> **Potential employees**
> If a company is keen to increase its talent pool of hires, creating content for them could really help that process. Content that showcases how employees enjoy working at the company, are given opportunities, and are celebrated and honoured for their good work, will demonstrate the happy company culture that exists there. This will help attract new employees with matching values and the right attitude to fit that culture.

2. What to post on the company page

A visitor to a company page can choose how they view the posts. They can toggle between viewing the most recent posts or the most engaged posts first. The exception to this is one selected post which can be pinned at the top. Apart from always securing new fresh content to signal this is an active page, your pinned post should work like a billboard for your core product or service to leave the visitor with no doubt about what the company offers.

It's hard enough as it is to get engagement on company page posts so a company posting dry and boring posts which only talk about its products is not helping itself. A company can, and should, direct people to the website for in-depth product information and use LinkedIn to showcase a different side of the company; the team, the culture, its personality. In order to start building a loyal customer base, it's important that companies help their customers get to know them. It's too easy for companies to forget that people buy from people.

On LinkedIn, thinking outside the box is key to staying ahead of the other 58 million companies on the platform!

In order to really attract people to, and keep them visiting, the company page, I urge companies to follow these guidelines:

> **Humanise the brand**
> People visiting the page will include customers, partners, employees, potential customers and investors. They want to know about the people within the organisation. They don't just want to read about 'what we do' or 'what we sell'. They want to feel a part of the brand and know what is happening inside the company.

>> **It's about time companies started looking at their followers and connections as their community, not just people to sell to**

People love stories of human behaviour and, by talking about these on the LinkedIn company page, a company will be differentiating themselves from their competitors as they showcase the uniqueness of their employees and how the company operates.

> **Address the problems the customers have**
By addressing the problems a company's audience has in relation to the type of product or service they offer will resonate with their audience. Talking about these problems, even without offering solutions, is a great way to make a connection with relevant people and potentially begin conversations around those topics. For example, posts on the company page for a project management tool could talk about how hard it is to be organised when you have a large event coming up. They could highlight different scenarios and begin a discussion about event planning in a company and how this could be made easier. This sort of post is ideal for getting employees leading the discussion on the page in the hope that those non-employees reading the post will join in too.

> **Involve the staff**
Asking staff to contribute posts is a sure-fire way to get them involved in the content strategy. It will also demonstrate to the world at large that the company is interested in what its staff have to say. Ideas such as 'why I love working for X' or 'a day in the life of…' will also give a deep insight into the culture and day to day workings of the company. People love stories, so, by publishing them on LinkedIn, a company has the potential to make a huge shift in the way in which its audience engages with its content.

- **Educate**
  Monitoring the reactions to content such as educational content can help a company identify who, in their audience, are potential clients. Thus these people can be subtly moved closer to the buying process. If a company is selling accounting software, for example, this could include advice about how people can manage their finances. In the wellness sector, it could be tips and tricks about how to look after yourself in certain situations.
- Who doesn't love a bit of free learning? Personal profiles are full of educational content - let's see more of it on company pages too. It shows that the company is interested in its audience and showcases the company as helpful and altruistic.

- **Talk about industry updates**
  Talking about policy changes, tech updates, legislation and other current events happening in the industry that could affect the audiences' lives will position a company as a 'go-to' place for important news and valuable information. This will in turn encourage their audience to follow the page and check in regularly for helpful information and industry updates.

- **Involve the audience in decision making**
  Asking opinions of their audience can help a company bring their audience closer by helping them feel involved in the brand. This can include gathering information to better help the company with its own marketing. It could even help a company to hone its offerings. Asking questions about why their audience like - or dislike - a particular offering could help develop its design or functionality.

This type of involvement can be light and fun as well as more serious. Questions about colours to use for branding, or which paint to use to decorate the office, for example, can encourage plenty of engagement as well as help the company get to know its audience.

These questions can be structured in the form of text posts or even better as polls, which generally have good engagement on LinkedIn.

> **Show social proof**
When preparing to go for dinner in a new town, I love reading reviews to help me choose where to go. If I'm buying a product online, I always check out not just the star ratings but the comments too. A company publishing client testimonials on LinkedIn is not only showing proof of their worth, they're also involving their clients in their marketing and giving them a voice.

> Testimonials are not showing off - they're showing proof. And that helps people make decisions

> **Talk about the different areas of the business**
Asking different team leaders to come up with content relevant to their department will help that content appeal to a wider audience. The tech team could create more technical content, sales teams could focus content around how customers are using the products and services, and the HR department could post tips about how they run an effective HR department. It doesn't have to be complicated.

Adding extra layers to the content is valid and helps the company produce content which is not just about the core products and services. By highlighting the different areas of the company, a company is making their content more varied. Content fatigue is real. A company can avoid this by keeping content fresh, interesting and wide ranging.

> **Involve the office pets**
If any employees have pets, including them in the company's marketing strategy will help position the company as caring, maybe even a bit quirky and certainly as having character! Very few people can resist a cute pet so it's worth trying. Take a look at LikeMind Media's company page. The office dog, Betty, makes regular and popular appearances.
I am aware that this strategy could be seen as being 'click bait' (i.e. just using something to get people to click), BUT - if you genuinely have a pet at your office, then it shows that you love pets - or at least yours.
Other people who also love their pets will enjoy talking about theirs - it's a commonality between you. In today's business world with potentially over a billion people scrolling around LinkedIn, let's embrace any form of conversation we can!

3. How often to post onto the company page?

LinkedIn reports that brands who post once a month gain followers 6x faster on their company page than those that keep a lower profile. But hey! you wouldn't be reading this book if you thought once a month was enough.

An article by Hubspot[31] highlighted that 2x a week is the optimal posting frequency on LinkedIn company pages, and not more than 1x a day.

In order to steadily build a following, being consistent is the key. Establishing a regular posting schedule is a far better approach than having flurries of posting activity followed by dry patches with no content going out. If a company has periods of time without posting, there is a possibility that their audience will forget about them and it's likely the algorithm will too, potentially leading to lower reach of posts and a reduction in brand awareness. All that work previously posting and engaging will have gone to waste.

Good quality posts 'stick around' on LinkedIn so timing of posts is less of a consideration than on other social media channels. Keeping an eye on the measurements of each post will help work out optimum posting days and times for you and your audience.

What time a company posts is of less importance than posting consistently. Stick around for the first 60-90 minutes to help get a conversation going and reply to comments

CHAPTER 6

Getting the company ready and excited to start

Every company has a different set of rules, systems and processes. What makes each company unique is the way it operates day to day. I strongly believe that yes, there may be rules, yes, there may be a formula to follow, but any new system being introduced into a company needs to work with, not against, its existing structure. I am a big fan of keeping this system as simple as possible while still reaping all of the benefits.

I work with companies of many different sizes, in many different industries, and in different ways but always to suit their needs. Yes, the framework is the same. But the skin on that framework is different for each company and each client. There is no right or wrong way to set up and run a system of employee advocacy. There are guidelines, but a company of 2,000 is going to run their system very differently from a company of five.

What would a system of employee advocacy look like for your company? What are some of the important considerations to make?

Legal implications

Employers have no legal jurisdiction over their employees' personal profiles or online engagement using their personal profiles. An employer cannot force their employees to engage on LinkedIn, or any other social media. Nor can they control the things that their employees talk about on social media or LinkedIn if the posting is done in the employees' own time.

There is an exception to this rule and that is if the employee has signed a contract to say they WILL engage on LinkedIn as part of their role. Before incorporating this into all future contracts, I would advise a company to bear certain things in mind:

> **Word the clause very carefully**
> A loosely worded contract, open to interpretation, will likely fall on the side of the employee if the lawyers get involved.

> **Offer a 'get-out' clause**
> It may be that the employee is not best placed to take part in the system of employee advocacy and a company would rather they didn't! Ensuring they have a water-tight 'get-out' clause will help either side to not feel an obligation to do this.

> **Don't make it obligatory**

A system of employee advocacy relies on the employees posting and engaging on LinkedIn because they want to. This desire will steer their communications and creativity on the platform. Someone who is being forced to communicate and create content is not going to do it with the passion and grace required - their reluctance will show. Forcing a reluctant employee to participate in an employee advocacy campaign could cause untold damage to a brand, as well as to the relationship with that employee.

Who should be in charge?

The ownership of running a system of employee advocacy often falls on the marketing department. In my experience, marketing departments are already stretched to their limits.

Having a person dedicated to run the system will give it a much greater chance of succeeding, as it will be their primary focus and will not get pushed aside by other priorities.

Whether a company uses someone external or they hire someone specifically for this job (which could be a part time role), or they change someone's role within the company, it's important that whoever is in charge has the capabilities to organise and coordinate the system.

It will also make it apparent to staff that this isn't just another initiative, it is a new part of the way the company operates. This will help give it the status it deserves and will help the onboarding and future success of the system.

The qualities of a good employee advocacy leader are:

- Having the gravitas and maturity to be a strong leader
- Having the ability to read, decipher and translate any analytics
- Having enough time to dedicate to making it a success
- Having empathy and patience
- Being organised and efficient
- Good communication skills
- Discretion

If the company has a dedicated social media or content creation department, it's important that the employee advocacy leader works closely with them.

A company should think carefully about whether to employ someone external to run the employee advocacy programme. A specialist may be better at defining the tasks and evaluating progression towards the set goals. It would be easy to put this project into the hands of someone who is drained already, or someone who does not have the skillset or the personality required to motivate and organise the employees to follow this through.

It may be worth considering hiring a fractional employee advocacy expert to train and work alongside an internal project leader. This could help ensure:

A. The system is robustly established
B. The system continues to operate after initial set up

How can teams be empowered to take part?

I always stress that the word is to 'empower' teams to take part. A sure way to help the system fail is to force people to do this. People who do things under duress do not do them well. There will be little creativity or commitment from those who are posting and commenting out of a feeling of obligation. It's important for companies to realise that each person is a representative of the company brand - we should never underestimate how expensive and time consuming it is to grow a brand message and how easy it is to ruin it.

There are countless examples of where an employee (including CEOs!) have ruined a brand by things they have said or done. You may remember Gerald Ratner's comment about the jewellery sold in his shops being 'rubbish'. What was supposed to be an amusing throw-away comment led to the demise of his multi-million pound brand, the dissolution of his company and his own bankruptcy. [32]

There are four key elements to empowering and growing the teams involved:

- Explaining the benefits of the system to ALL employees in order to onboard the right people for the right reasons
- Providing thorough training and support the whole way through the process
- Ensuring the information required by each person is simple to access and utilise. If there are too many steps or it's too complicated, there will be a high level of drop out

> Ensuring each person is 'themselves' at all times and that they show their own personality on the platform. If someone is trying to put on a 'corporate voice', their writing will be stiff and jarring

Employee advocacy is not a system that can be set up and run by itself. It needs to be continuously monitored, evaluated and improved to ensure its success. Otherwise, it will fail.

On average, it takes more than two months before a new behaviour becomes automatic - 66 days to be exact. In a study by Lally, it took anywhere from 18-254 days for people to form a new habit[33]

Communication up front is key to the ongoing success of any new system. If a company doesn't communicate the requirements of what is involved, what the system means to the company and what it could mean to each employee, teams will not trust the system. Managing the expectations of employees before they take part is key.

Bringing in a new way of selling and communicating can meet resistance, so a company should bring their teams onboard as early as possible with as much information as they can provide.

How should advocates be selected?

It will not be appropriate for everyone in the team to take part in the system of employee advocacy. Choosing the right advocates or ambassadors should be given careful consideration.

- Some people may want to take part, but they may be unable to do so due to time restrictions
- Not all employees will be suited to representing the company on LinkedIn
- There will be team members who resist going on LinkedIn - but with a bit of clever training and nurturing they 'get it' and could well prove to be valuable assets

I like to work with the team lead (usually marketing or CEO) to help identify who may do this well.

The most important supporters are:

- The sales team. This is a must! Especially team leaders who can encourage their team or teams.
- Those in technical roles. The public loves a bit of technical product knowledge, and who better to talk about that side of things than the people who are immersed in it? The technical team may not need to be as active on LinkedIn as some of the others but it would be good to involve them and encourage them to share their knowledge.
- CEO and leadership team. Leading by example, having the CEO active on LinkedIn is a great motivator for the rest of the company.

See how Dougie Loan of Source Whale appears on LinkedIn. His content, and the way he engages with his audience, positions him as a caring and forward thinking CEO.

As a starting point, my advice is to utilise all those employees who are customer facing and who are used to communicating with the public. Then look at other departments to see if the company can show a broader range of employees on LinkedIn.

Selecting the right individuals for your employee advocacy programme is crucial for its success. Here are some criteria to consider when choosing participants from each team:

> **Enthusiastic and engaged employees**
> Staff who are genuinely enthusiastic about their work and engaged with the company, who have a passion and positivity which can be infectious. Their advocacy efforts will be authentic, and this will show in their communication.

> **Diverse representatives**
> Any advocacy team should include individuals from different departments, roles, and levels within the organisation. This diversity can provide a well-rounded perspective and help reach a broader audience.

> **Strong communicators**
> Individuals who are effective communicators, both in person and online, and who are comfortable expressing themselves, sharing insights, and interacting with their networks.

> **Knowledgeable about the company**

Employees who have a good understanding of the company's products, services, values and overall mission will be better able to communicate this information effectively and authentically on LinkedIn.

> **Active on social media**
> At least 90% of employees are likely to already be active on social media platforms. Participants should be comfortable using social media and, of course, LinkedIn to share content and engage with their networks.

> **Positive influencers**
> Employees who have a positive influence on their peers may be able to sway opinions and are more likely to be effective advocates for the company.

> **Leadership potential**
> Employees with leadership potential are likely to inspire and train others in the company to take part. This will not only benefit the current efforts but also may build a pipeline for leadership development.

> **Tech-savvy individuals**
> Since employee advocacy often involves digital products or platforms, individuals who are tech-savvy and comfortable using the necessary tools for advocacy efforts will be useful to have on the programme.

> **Team players**
> Collaboration is key in advocacy programmes, and individuals who can work effectively with others can enhance the overall impact of the initiative.

> **Supportive management**
> Having strong leadership and support from the top of the organisation is crucial for encouraging participation and ensuring that employees have the time and resources to engage in advocacy activities.

> **Willingness to learn and adapt**
> The digital landscape and best practices for advocacy may evolve, so having employees who are willing to stay informed and adjust their approach accordingly is beneficial for its continued success.

> **Alignment with company values**
> Employees whose values align with those of the company are likely to ensure that their advocacy efforts are authentic and consistent with the organisation's overall messaging.

By carefully selecting employees based on these criteria, a company can build a diverse and effective team for the employee advocacy programme. If run effectively, it's likely that other employees will start to see the benefits and request to be considered also.

Which tools should be used?

Internal communication is going to be a vital part of the success of this system. Having a safe space to share information, ideas, content, diary information etc will be the key to its success.

Here are some accessible tools which will help:

- **LinkedIn groups**
  Setting up a LinkedIn group is easy to do and they are pretty straightforward to run. The feed of a group is purely linear, so whilst it's easy to follow, it's not so easy to find old messages. Of course, it relies on people actually logging into LinkedIn to check the group - which could be a positive or negative attribute.

- **Slack**
  If a company is already using Slack, it can easily be used to categorise content to be shared and to divide content into subjects or groups. It's also possible to store documents and share posts which you would like employees to either post or repost. Slack can also be used to share clickable links to posts to encourage teams to engage with them. I would suggest only using Slack if the teams are already familiar with it, as giving the team another new thing to learn may lead to resistance and either a lower initial uptake or drop out.

- **Google Drive**
  This is one of my favourite tools as it's easy to store things such as images, schedules, diaries, and ideas. Most people know how to access and share a Google Drive folder. The content manager could put posts in different folders depending on the team splits. Assisted by having email notifications switched on, a drive folder can prompt swift action when posts go live.

- **Project management tools**

Asana, Monday, Trello or similar tools can be used for all the above functions. If a company is already using one of these, it would make sense to continue. These tools could be used on their own or in conjunction with a Google Drive folder or even a LinkedIn group.

> **Employee advocacy platforms**
> There are also platforms which specialise in employee advocacy programmes across LinkedIn and social media channels. If a company is thinking of choosing a tool designed for the employee advocacy system, I advise speaking to their trainer/consultant first. If they are bringing in a consultant to run the employee advocacy programme, it would be sensible to choose a platform the trainer is familiar with. Also many third party tools will only work with larger companies - some with a minimum of 200 participants. Bear in mind that these tools, while new to a team, are definitely worth investigating as they are designed specifically for this purpose and therefore are designed to make everyone's job easier and provide invaluable insights into results.

> **The 'My Company' tab**
> The 'My Company' tab is available on all company pages of companies with over 10 employees on LinkedIn. It is an employee-only community where employees can communicate with each other. It is a place where employees can see up-to-date information and news about their company. There is a 'trending coworker' tab where employees can see what their colleagues are posting.

The person in charge of the employee advocacy programme can put posts in the tab for employees to share on their personal profiles. They can even now get analytics on employee behaviour. It is also possible to share posts from other accounts on LinkedIn which they feel employees could comment on.

So, as far as an employee advocacy programme is concerned, the 'My Company' tab could be a fantastic help to keep the system alive, keep employees engaged and keep an eye on everyone.

I advise anyone running an employee advocacy system to check it out and see if it works for them as it could make life much easier and really help the employee advocacy programme succeed.

One of the most important factors to create a successful employee advocacy system is that it's easily accessible to everyone involved

Choosing the right trainer

So what's next?

The company is ready to go!

- Legals sorted
- Budget identified
- Someone appointed to run it
- A system chosen and set up, ready to facilitate
- Employees and C Suite are excited to learn more

The next step is to train those excited and empowered employees how to get started.

I've talked about the importance of getting the system established correctly for it to succeed. A company should not underestimate the value of ensuring that every participant or potential participant has adequate training.

> **You've heard the phrase 'knowledge is power' - in this case 'knowledge is empowerment'**

When people understand the 'why' as well as the 'how' to approach LinkedIn, there is an immediate transformation!

When I explain the psychology around LinkedIn, it is often a 'eureka' moment for many of my clients, and brings about a huge shift in their learning and activity on LinkedIn.

A company should never underestimate the value of fully training their teams to empower them to maximise their time, and use the platform efficiently to produce the best results.

I work with companies over a full day of training or a series of three online workshops to help all employees who have opted in to join the programme. It's a process which involves three main aspects:

1. How to build a personal profile to establish each employee as a thought leader in their area of expertise
2. How to promote content from the company page and create new content for personal profiles
3. Social selling and lead generation

In one day with up to 30 employees, it's possible to make huge changes in mindset as well as skills.

My advice to a company is shop around to find a LinkedIn trainer who has trained companies in employee advocacy before. The best person is someone who understands and is passionate about realising the benefits of employee advocacy. This person will be able to share their enthusiasm in a way that should rub off on at least some of the team.

An experienced employee advocacy trainer fully understands the needs of the company and each individual employee. They will understand that different roles in the organisation will behave differently on the platform, will be aware of relationships among the teams, and that employees are promoting themselves as well as the company. The way employees set up their profiles and behave on LinkedIn is different from job seekers and entrepreneurs and this fact shouldn't be underestimated; it's important that the company chooses a LinkedIn trainer who is also aware of this.

What questions should a company ask when choosing a person to train their team?

- **Does the person have a full understanding of how company pages operate?**

- **Is it clearly stated in their profile that they teach employee advocacy?**

- **Will they support the company after the initial training?**
  In order to capitalise on the initial investment of training, most companies, after the initial success

and enthusiasm generated during the training, need help to harness and continue the programme.

> **Are they a fit in terms of location?**
Is it possible to get all the team together for the training or does it need someone who can train staff remotely, or even run a training session in a hybrid way - with some people in the room and some on screen? What would be the logistics of keeping a person on as a consultant if they don't live nearby?

> **How have they worked before?**
It's always worth asking any potential trainers or consultants how they're used to working and what brings the most success for the companies they work with.

> **Are they the right 'fit' for your company culture?**
A company should make sure that the trainer's teaching aligns with their teams. A couple of meetings with relevant members of staff should answer this question, but it's always worth finding out the approach adopted by the trainer. A company may have a workforce who prefers a more sombre approach or it may be that the team likes a bit more fun in their learning. Getting this wrong could be the difference between a successful employee advocacy system, and one where the employees don't engage at all.

> **Does the trainer provide learning materials?**
Some kind of workbook or learning tools can be useful to help the team. Are these included in the package and in what form are they delivered - print, online, or both? Ironing out niggly things like this can

help the process run smoothly and contribute to its success.

> **How many people do they teach at one time?**
Too many people in one workshop could de-personalise a training and make it far too long. Ensuring everyone attending is fully engaged all the way through is key to the initial adoption rate.

> **Do they provide workshop or seminar style training?**
What happens in the training? Is it a workshop style where people are taking action with the trainer present? Or is it more of a seminar style where the employees are given the information and then they go away and implement it on their own? What is the best type of training for the workforce? Are they self motivated enough to 'do their homework'? Or would it make more sense to get the work done all together in the room with everyone, including the trainer for support and accountability?

PART 3
TRAINING THE TEAMS

The company page is now all complete, fully optimised with relevant keywords and phrases, and ready to receive all those potential new visitors.

The teams are fully appraised and the relevant people have been chosen. This amazing group of forward thinking early adopters have been fully onboarded. They've connected with their trainer and they are ready to start their new LinkedIn journey.

In this section, I will cover the three main steps to LinkedIn success for an employee:

1. Building a profile that appeals to ideal clients and customers (chapter 7)
2. Creating and sharing content (chapter 8)
3. Outreach and social selling (chapter 9)

CHAPTER 7

Employees' personal profiles

Building their own personal profile will begin to position each employee as their own personal brand. Our personal profiles are our shop windows, they are the representation of who we are, and often the first touch point someone has with us - so we need to make them count!

I am often asked how 'personal' employees should be on LinkedIn. I will always encourage employers to allow their employees to be 'themselves' on LinkedIn, while bearing in mind they are also representing the company. The overarching philosophy remains, that those who have taken part in the system should be encouraged to be themselves.

If the team is empowered and encouraged to shine, speak freely and position themselves as experts in their area of expertise, they are more likely to embrace the system and enjoy it. This will encourage them to come to LinkedIn with enthusiasm rather than seeing it as a duty which needs to be fulfilled.

Knowing WHO it is they're speaking to will help each employee position their profile accordingly. Who each person's audience is will influence things like what they wear in their profile photo, how they write their headline and about section, which hashtags they use, what they talk about and, of course, how they say it.

I encourage each participant to focus on their own relevant audience. Think of LinkedIn as a complicated road system. If each employee starts from a different point and travels along their own route, as they navigate their journey, they will meet people along the way. If this approach can be followed by several employees, they will each build their own network of friends and connections, their own separate audiences. If each employee stays in their own lane, communicating and connecting with people who can help them on their journey, their road will be much smoother and their efforts better rewarded.

You may have noticed I said 'everyone' should set up their personal profiles. Whether or not people are taking part in the employee advocacy programme, if the company has the resources, I strongly advise that even the profiles of those not taking part are updated - even if it's only the main sections as outlined in this book.

Creating all the personal profiles to have a congruent design and message will do three primary things:

1. **Increase the reach of the company page**
   Including keywords in the personal profiles of employees will help their profiles come up higher in search results on LinkedIn, and on Google as well. This will help drive more traffic to the company page as well as, potentially, to the website.

2. **Further strengthen the company brand**
   If all the personal profiles have a similar look, feel and tone of voice, it shows a strength of branding which helps build recognition and trust among their audience. After working with me, the whole team at FANATTIK optimised their profiles with 'same-style' photos, even though not all of them are participants of the employee advocacy scheme. Such consistent presentation helps people recognise the brand when they first visit the company page.

3. **Show cohesion among the company**
   Having all employees' profiles updated also shows that the company cares about their teams. It also shows that the employees are a cohesive team pulling together for the greater good of the company as well as its clients and customers.

Why are LinkedIn profiles so important?

It's relatively easy to share your LinkedIn profile when meeting people at events, but most of our connections and followers come via the platform itself. I know this as I'm pretty sure I haven't met even half of my almost 17,000 (at time of writing) followers face to face!

When someone is browsing their LinkedIn feed and sees a comment or a post they like from someone they don't know, it's an easy click-through to the person's profile. That is the first step in deciding whether or not to connect with or follow the person.

A good profile does three things:

1. It clearly and concisely informs the visitor exactly what that person does, how they work and who they work with
2. It tells the person's story in a relevant and engaging way
3. It enables the person to be found in keyword searches across LinkedIn and Google

At the time of writing there are potentially 36 different sections to our personal profiles. Yes, 36! LinkedIn is presenting us with a fantastic opportunity to showcase ourselves and position ourselves as thought leaders in our industries, whether we're employees, business owners, students, or job seekers.

Don't waste this amazing opportunity!

LinkedIn profiles are such a huge piece of our marketing material that we don't want to get them wrong. For many, LinkedIn will be their ONLY marketing material.

Optimising personal profiles

Without going into fine details about the 36 different sections of a LinkedIn personal profile, I would like to focus on the five main sections for each employee.

1. Banner or background image

I advise employees to use the company page banner - or an adapted version of it. This will ensure cohesion and strength of branding as well as keeping things simple for each employee.

Company page banners are a different size from personal profile banners so I recommend having something designed which is perhaps a bit more 'human' than the company banner, but which unmistakably links the page and all the profiles.

Some employees may resist this and prefer to use their own banner. However, they may be happy with having the company logo or designing the banner so it's part personal and part company. Of course their decision must be accepted, whatever they decide.

2. Profile photos

As outlined above when I mentioned the profile photos of FANATTIK, I advise having cohesion here so try to style all the profile photos in a similar way. It would be good to start with a clean slate and encourage everyone to have a new photo to kick off the employee advocacy campaign. Consider hiring a photographer to take all the new photos.

When I run corporate training sessions, if the teams don't have up-to-date photos, I either bring in a photographer during the session or I get them to take each other's photographs just using each other's phones.

With some guidance the results can be great, especially if there are design elements in and around the office or studio which could be used as backgrounds. For example, Matt Beatty of Fibo and some of his team use their different panel designs as their backdrops.

It's important to remember to get new hires to update their profiles on joining the company so the cohesion isn't lost.

3. Headline

Our headline travels with us all around LinkedIn - well, the first third or so does. Whenever we post or comment on a post, that first third of our headline sits right below our name.

> **What is written in the first third of our headline could be the difference between someone clicking through to find out more about us - or not**

Too many people make the mistake of leading with their job title. I get it, it's secure and functional. It's also usually not what people care about. It doesn't say anything about what they actually DO.

For example, when meeting someone at an in-person event, if they said they were 'CEO of Smith and Jones', what does that tell you about them? It says they're in charge - but of what? You have no idea if they are someone you may need in your life or even where to take the conversation. You may think it rude to then ask 'who are Smith and Jones?' Feeling wrong-footed or insecure that early on in a relationship is not going to help build that all-important trust. Saying what we do, or what the company does, in our headline is a far better start.

> **Don't be vanilla! The chances are that there are hundreds of people out there on LinkedIn doing a very similar job as you. Stand out, be different**

Talk about the problems that you solve for your clients, share a bit of knowledge or your thoughts. Your LinkedIn headline is the first piece of text where you can differentiate yourself from your competition and position yourself as an expert who helps people with a specific problem - and there are only 220 characters so don't waste them!

Here's a structure you could follow:

I work with/help [TYPE OF CUSTOMERS]

To or feel [WHAT DO YOU DO FOR THEM OR HOW DO YOU MAKE THEM FEEL?]

We're different because [HOW ARE YOU DIFFERENT FROM YOUR COMPETITORS?]

As you're talking about the company, it is acceptable to use 'WE' instead of 'I' and speak for the company as a whole - even though this is your personal profile. What you're doing is presenting yourself as a team member who, with your colleagues, solves the problems you've identified.

The final sentence, or third, should focus on why you or your company is different from your competitors. What is the special ingredient you/your company brings? THIS is your USP (unique selling proposition) and needs to be highlighted to separate your company from the competition.

4. About section

This is where people can talk in more detail about what the company does but also what they themselves do.

Lead with two or three main problems that you solve for your clients and identify how you solve those problems. This will ensure that you demonstrate a solid understanding of your clients needs and can identify their problems before they've even come to you. This will really resonate with your ideal clients.

The About section on personal profiles is a great place to 'sell' the company. Tell the readers what you love about working for the company, what makes you go to work every day. This could be tangible things such as the fact that the company is doing pioneering work, or they're kind and helpful to you as an employee. Employees can also introduce some humour here, if appropriate. Identifying quirks of their colleagues - without being detrimental obviously - will help personalise the About section and potentially help people feel closer to the brand.

Each employee should highlight their specific role within the company and what they do - always bearing in mind who they want to attract. Bear in mind the language that you use should be easily understandable by your audience. Many people make the mistake of using 'industry speak' to try to sound authoritative. It only goes to confuse those who don't use that language, and make them feel insecure.

Some short testimonials can be used here if there is space, and finally a call to action. This could be to 'find out more' (add website information) or 'get in touch' (add email address).

Don't forget to use keywords and phrases when writing profiles. These are the words and phrases that people will use when searching for the goods or services of the company.

Finally I would emphasise the need to allow space when constructing the About section. Don't just present a huge wall of text that nobody will want to spend time reading. Use headings and spread out the text.

Emojis are now a very powerful tool on LinkedIn and they come in all shapes and colours. There are some very subtle ones as well as bright purple and orange hearts! Choose a small selection that each member of the company uses over and over. This way they'll become part of the brand message. If you visit Source Whale's employee profiles, you will see they use only blue emojis. They began by embracing the blue whale emoji and I encouraged them to use different blue emojis to keep the consistency and further heighten the brand recognition.

5. Experience section

The Experience section is where we list previous jobs we have had. From an employee perspective, it's important to ensure this is up to date. Forgetting to update that they've moved to a new company here will imply that the person is not up to speed with LinkedIn or that they don't really care about their public image.

From an employer's perspective too, it's advantageous for employees to add the new position and connect their profile to the company page. Employee growth is one sign of a company's success and LinkedIn now shows the number of employees on the company page as a 'bracket' 1-10/11-50 etc.

Also, if the company wants to talk about its employees on the company page, having them connected to the page ensures they can be tagged in on posts. It also goes a long way to making the organisation look more professional. The more personal connections a company has via its employees, the more likely the company is to get found on LinkedIn. So the more employees linked to the page, potentially the more visibility a company has.

Likewise, when someone is about to leave a company, they should be encouraged to remove the link to the company page as this could blur the brand message and make the company page look out of date.

CHAPTER 8

Creating content on personal profiles

Usually the first step in teaching employees about posting on LinkedIn is to spread the message that fresh content is not about re-inventing the wheel each time. We don't always have to showcase ourselves as thought leaders and experts with insights to wow our audiences; it doesn't have to be complicated and high brow.

Not all employees will feel comfortable posting their own content on LinkedIn. Those that don't want to publish original content should not be made to feel guilty or bad about this. I praise any activity, however small, in an attempt to foster a positive environment where people do as much as they can. Some employees will only ever comment or like the posts on the company page but there will always be some who will be happy to push themselves out of their comfort zones. This obviously should be encouraged and supported.

Three types of content for personal profiles

There are three ways in which employees can create posts:

- By creating fresh content to post on their personal profiles and/or the company page
- Curating posts from the company website or from external sources
- Taking the company page posts and posting them on their own profiles

1. Creating fresh content

I often work with people who have never posted anything on LinkedIn. The most common objection I hear is 'fear'. Fear of looking stupid, fear of saying the wrong thing but the biggest fear of all is that of being judged - by their peers, bosses, friends or previous colleagues. While I understand that fear, the truth is that most people are so impressed that someone has actually posted that the feedback is almost universally positive.

I will never forget the first time I posted on LinkedIn. I felt physically sick with nerves as I hit 'publish'. Guess what happened? Nothing! Well, that's not quite true. I got a client! Yes, someone I had met a few years previously saw my first LinkedIn post and enquired about some social media training, then subsequently engaged me to train him and his team!

We all start with zero connections and not a clue how to use the platform. Progress takes time, I tell people when I'm training them, so take it slowly and move just - and yes, just - outside your comfort zone.

Each ambassador will have a very different attitude to posting - and each should be embraced. Content can be created in so many different ways and about such a variety of subjects, putting up posts can appeal to a wide variety of ambassadors with mixed skills and mindsets. Some ambassadors will want to write long form blogs, others will be more comfortable posting selfies of themselves at events, and yet others will feel happier curating content from other people's blogs, and posting those. Any interaction with LinkedIn is great and, again, to be encouraged.

Let's have a look at the kinds of things employees can post about on LinkedIn:

- **Work-place events - corporate days out and even LinkedIn training days**
  It's easy to take a quick group photo and post it on LinkedIn. It helps show that the company invests in the wellness and growth of its employees.

- **Conferences or trade shows**
  Be sure to tag in the conference organiser and any colleagues. Again, a quick selfie and some text will usually suffice - simple! Obviously a post can be longer and more complex but generally, a post showing that colleagues are or have been at a trade show is simply a brand awareness exercise. It can also serve to invite others to join them if they're at the show. These posts should not be over-complicated.

> **New products or services**
> Talking about new products from a personal perspective will resonate more closely than just talking about their specifications. A photo or short film showing the product, just taken with a phone, can be more appealing to viewers than a slick, expensive corporate video. Packaging and shipping company, Cargowise Solutions does this really well when showing their paper shredding or packaging machines.

> **Photo at their desk**
> It's less common for people to work in the office now, so a photo showing that an employee is in the office tells a story. They could even talk about their journey to and from work. What does their home desk look like? Is there a cat sitting on a keyboard? Humanising the content will go a long way to drawing the audience closer.

> **Client stories**
> Sharing a client success story is great content. This can be done from the company page as well as from relevant employees' profiles. Always seek a client's permission - and endeavour to get a photo with the client to post, too. Posts with faces almost always get the highest engagement.

> **Industry updates and insights**
> Employees who show that they're up to date with current trends or politics around their industry are positioning themselves as experts. This type of post will need more thought and will probably take longer but can reap amazing results.

> **Original thought leadership pieces**
> Again, this type of content is not for everyone but should be encouraged if someone is keen.

Each person will write their posts using their own language and emphasising what is important to them. Encouraging autonomy will help this process evolve. Don't stifle the creativity involved in this process - embrace the fact that everyone is learning and growing.

As an example of how autonomy can help the process, let's say three employees attend a trade show together and they all want to post about it. They each could take a 'selfie' and talk about their own experience of the event in their post. A range of diverse voices will help to make content more interesting, and the fact that it will appear on three people's feeds, not just one, ensures the reach is increased.

Here's a cheeky idea for some trade show content - get a photo of you / your team with an ideal client - or two. Post it on your profile and tag them in. Tagging them in a post after the event will help them remember you!

2. Curating posts from the website or from other external sources

The good news is that it's not necessary to create fresh content every single time you post. There is also a place on LinkedIn for sharing content written by other experts, from other publications or even the company website.

A word of warning here, these posts will always need the link to the item of content you're sharing so, on that basis, the reach of these posts may be lower than other posts. This is because the LinkedIn algorithm does not favour external links. This makes sense as LinkedIn wants people to stay on the platform rather than leave to read content elsewhere.

Curating posts from external sources does several things:

- If you don't have time to post a piece of original content, it's still better than not posting at all
- It puts you in front of the author and/or publication of the curated content (as long as you tag them in)
- It shows your audience that you're keeping your finger on the pulse of what's happening in your industry
- It gives you a chance to add some thought leadership of your own without having to publish a huge long blog or newsletter

When you have found an article you would like to curate onto your feed, whether it's from the company website or any external source, these are the steps:

- Copy the URL of the page from the bar at the top
- Go to LinkedIn and start creating a post
- Paste the link into the box, you will see the image automatically populates too - win win!
- Add your thoughts above the link - what is it about this post that you like, why do you think your readers will find it interesting?
- Tag in the author, the publication and any other contributors
- Add 3-5 relevant hashtags and post!

It really is that simple!

The strategy for some people is to ONLY find and post relevant articles from others. It's not perfect but it's better than not posting at all!

3. Posting company page posts on personal profiles

> **Posting on personal profiles can potentially give a post up to 561% more reach than the same post on a company page**

I said this before but it's worth saying again, this is a statistic from LinkedIn, therefore we need to pay attention to what it's telling us. If a post goes out on a LinkedIn company page, it will get seen only by a tiny fraction of those who follow the page. To really give that post some chance of being seen, get the same post out on the personal profiles of the employees. It sounds simple enough, doesn't it?

It is! If one or some of the ambassadors take the same content as on the company page - copy the text and image and create a whole new post for their own feeds, it will be seen by a much larger, and different, audience.

This requires a much lower level of effort than creating a fresh piece of content from scratch, and it does reap benefits.

The main objection I hear is 'what if someone sees the same post several times?'

Apart from the fact that this is unlikely, what if that does happen? Let me state an example: Are you cross or annoyed by the fact that I have already mentioned that:

> **Posting on personal profiles can potentially give a post up to 561% more reach than the same post on a company page**

Yes, I am aware that I've now written this three times now in this book! Why? Because you're much more likely to remember it when repeated multiple times. And you had probably forgotten where you'd seen it the first time.

The next time you're driving down the motorway and you see that yellow 'M", do you feel annoyed that McDonald's are spamming you, or do you feel like you want a burger? The next time that song comes on that you know the lyrics to, do you want to turn off the radio, or do you sing along with a bit of happy nostalgia floating around your brain?

Seeing the same content multiple times makes it familiar. And as I have said three times now, the chances are that most people won't see it from the company page. Posting company page content on personal profiles as well is such a simple strategy and one which I don't see used enough on LinkedIn.

The secret to getting the best results here is to post the same posts on personal profiles and pages at different times and on different days. Recent and limited research suggests the posts should go out on the company page first, then a day or two later they should start going out on personal profiles.

Putting them all out at the same time may confuse the algorithm and lead to low levels of engagement.

How to write a post to engage your audience

One of the biggest struggles people have with LinkedIn, and one which deters people from using the platform, is how to express themselves. Whilst LinkedIn is a business platform, the key is to be ourselves at all times. 'Authentic' is a buzzword at the time of writing but it is so for good reason. In the words of my good friend, Timea Kadar, 'Your USP*[34] is you'.

Employees should be encouraged to show their personalities in their language. I cannot stress enough how LinkedIn is about building relationships. If people cannot be themselves on the platform, other people don't have a chance to get to know them. So I encourage people to 'write like they speak'. This also ensures that they feel comfortable with what they are writing. Even if someone's writing isn't perfect, as long as it can be understood then, in most cases, it is acceptable.

I have worked with people whose language came across as a little inappropriate or inflammatory. With a little support, we realised that it came out of fear of not knowing how to express themselves. We identified that their written word did not reflect the way they communicated verbally. With a little guidance, this was ironed out.

More recently, I worked with a company where one of the employees was mildly dyslexic. He was, understandably, nervous about posting on LinkedIn. We realised that this nervousness could be overcome in two ways. One was to encourage him to use video instead of written posts where possible, and secondly to mention his dyslexia in his headline and be up front about it. The minute he had been 'given permission' to be himself, we saw his confidence grow, as well as his following on LinkedIn!

Despite the fact that there are over a billion personal profiles on LinkedIn at the time of writing, less than 2% of those post regularly on LinkedIn.[35] This is optimistic news for those people who ARE posting, as the chances are that their content will get seen and, depending on how they structure and post their content, it will get seen by the right people.

Ideally, every company will have at least one person who wants to reinforce and grow their own thought leadership. This is likely to be, but does not have to be, the CEO. A company of thought leaders is a force to be reckoned with - on LinkedIn or anywhere. If there are just three people within the organisation posting value-adding, interesting and entertaining content on LinkedIn and even across other social platforms, the impact of that for the company as a whole could be staggering! Factor that in with the opportunities which could arise for each of those people. Just imagine how much the company's name and its reputation could grow exponentially until it becomes THE company on everyone's lips.

If an employee really wishes to position themselves as a thought leader, it is important to continuously and consistently appear in people's feeds with original, interesting and relevant content.

How often to post on personal profiles?

There is not a finite number of times anyone 'should' post on personal profiles. We are aware that posting more than once in a 24 hour period is detrimental to the engagement on the posts.

As with company page posts, the key for each person to grow their audience is to be consistent.

It doesn't have to take all day either. Let's imagine a company with 30 employees plus the CEO and CMO posting on LinkedIn. If each person posted once a month, that's more than one post a day going out on LinkedIn representing the company! That is potentially pretty powerful.

I would suggest starting slowly and see if each person could get into the habit of posting once a week or a fortnight, (bi-weekly to those of you in the States).

Quality over quantity here though, so no employee should be made to feel this is an obligation. What is more important at the start is to get each employee feeling confident about using the platform. The last thing you want is to go out all guns blazing initially and then run out of ideas and energy. It's so much more powerful to build a posting schedule consistently and slowly, which will evolve with the person's increasing confidence and audience.

CHAPTER 9

Increasing the reach of the company page posts

When a post is first published on LinkedIn, the algorithm picks it up and circulates it to a very tiny section of the connections or followers of that page or profile. If that post then gets a lot of engagement in the first 90 minutes or so of being published, it will get pushed out to more people.

What LinkedIn wants is to keep people on the platform, and the best way of doing that is to make sure that what LinkedIn puts in their feeds is what users like. This makes sense, right? If people like the content on the platform, the more they will use the platform and the more likely they will be to spend money to enhance their experience while using it.

If, on the second journey around LinkedIn, the post gets good engagement again, the algorithm will push it out to an even wider audience.

A post will start to get comments and likes, first from first degree connections, and then as time goes on, from second and even third+ degree connections. That's when you know that your post is being pushed out way beyond your own network. LinkedIn will keep on doing this until engagement levels start to fall.

So, how can a company use this information to its advantage?

Answer: by encouraging the ambassadors to react to the content on the company page and also on each others' posts within the first 90 minutes of being posted.

There are several ways this can be done depending on time and resources.

The best engagement strategies

There are several ways a team can engage with company page posts, but they don't all have the same impact. I give them a star rating to illustrate a system of efficacy.

☆ Reacting

Reacting with a like, celebration, support, love, insightful, or funny emoji is the minimum type of engagement - aside from doing nothing, of course. Reacting to posts potentially helps the post get more reach and helps show that post to the employees' followers and connections.

☆ **Reposting**

Research by LinkedIn expert Richard Van Der Blom suggests that reposting posts does help their engagement, even if there are no comments added. However, I am still only going to give this one star as simply reposting without adding a comment (see below), does not give any context to the post and is unlikely to encourage anyone to read it.

☆ ☆ **Reposting with your thoughts**

When we share a piece of news, it's valuable to put it in context so in my mantra of 'treating LinkedIn as if it were a real life situation' I am a strong believer we should do this on LinkedIn too.

Giving people a reason to read the shared post, pointing out any benefits they may get from it, is likely to encourage them to read it. By adding your thoughts you can enthuse people, give them a reason to click and spend two minutes of their time reading.

Imagine if you were sitting next to someone and you thought they'd like to read the article you've just finished, it's unlikely that you would simply put it under their nose without telling them why you think they would enjoy it. It's a small effort to add your personal touch to make the experience relevant for your audience.

☆ ☆ ☆ **Commenting on the post itself**

I have explained how LinkedIn rewards posts which receive high levels of engagement when they're first posted. If employees can comment on a post within the first 90 minutes of posting, it will help the post get better engagement.

On another level, if people reading the posts see that the employees are engaging in the content, it could send a positive message about what a close community exists there.

Employees can use the company page posts to start chatting to their colleagues as if they were in the office together. They can begin to create 'banter' as well as more serious thought-provoking conversations around the content.

Treating the LinkedIn company page as if it was the boardroom or the office reception, could encourage comments from those outside the company as well as show what a close community is being built in this company.

☆ ☆ ☆ ☆ ☆ ☆ ☆ ☆ **Create a duplicate post**

Want to know how to get 10 points? Yes, by re-creating the post on personal profiles! I talked earlier about the power of taking the post text and copying it into a post on a personal profile and using the same image too. It's such a simple strategy and can increase that reach enormously.

In fact, employees don't have to limit themselves to one of these things, they can do a combination of two or more strategies in less than a minute.

Maximising employee engagement on company page posts

Obviously, all increased activity on the company and personal profiles is helpful. In order to maximise the benefits and ensure this system has a chance of great success, everyone should know when the posts are to be posted on the page in advance. This will allow employees to put aside 5 or 10 minutes to engage on the posts whilst they are fresh in the feed.

This is where using a dedicated portal could help. The posts could be placed in the portal in advance for teams to take a look at and craft really effective comments. This takes some thought and planning but if there are big thought leadership posts or posts by the CEO, this could really help increase their reach. For the employees to be able to plan responses to multiple posts at once is likely to also make the task more manageable, and more employees are likely to engage. If they are involved in planning and suggesting upcoming topics, even more so. It may be relevant to suggest ideas of what employees could include in those comments, to give them the confidence to comment - especially when the system is in its early stages.

It won't be appropriate for everyone to comment on every post, so by dividing the advocates into teams and only allocating relevant posts to each team, it will keep the system efficient and help make it more attainable for each employee.

How employees can best support each other's posts

If a company has been lucky enough to empower employees from different departments, they can create clear groups of advocates who can post about different themes and subjects. I advise mixing seniority within the groups. A department head commenting on a post by an intern can help amplify that post and give that intern a huge confidence boost. It will also showcase the company as having a good internal communications strategy, as well as an appreciation for young talent. Both of which are positive outcomes for the company!

What is vital here is that all the communications on the company page and on the employee's personal profiles must remain genuine and authentic. If posts begin to look like they're written by the marketing department the system will start to crumble.

If using strategies like the ones I've outlined causes the content to look stilted, if they're leading the employees to feel insecure or nervous about what to post and how to comment, then the whole process should be readdressed. If there are too many rules, the system could look manufactured and artificial. This system is about free flowing and diverse communication and that should be nurtured and not quashed by a set of rules.

I know. It can seem overwhelming. Having an external lead involved from the start could help keep this system manageable for the company. The more manageable it is from the start, the more likely it is to succeed.

CHAPTER 10

Outreach and Social selling

With over half of the world's population on social media, it's no surprise that using social networks to sell our products and services is a strategy that all sales and marketing teams need to employ.

> **56% of sales people utilise social media to find potential prospects**[36]

> **80% of B2B leads coming from social media are from LinkedIn**[37]

This means that if a company is not using LinkedIn for its lead generation, it's potentially leaving money on the table.

I am asked almost weekly by potential clients whether they should also be on other social media platforms. I usually reply with 'Where are your clients hanging out?'

Go to where your clients and potential clients are. Focus on what works, and in nearly all cases with B2B lead generation, what works is LinkedIn.

Where many fail is that LinkedIn is not a numbers game where we shout our message as loud as we can at as many people as we can, and hope it sticks somewhere.

I hope at this point, you'll agree that LinkedIn is all about building relationships, showing our faces, ideas and personalities consistently, and adding value to people.

A complaint about LinkedIn which I hear increasingly is that people are getting far too many salesy messages. Usually these come in the form of Inmails. Inmails are used by people who have the paid version of LinkedIn (Premium) to send messages without sending a connection request.

My default button is to 'reject' all Inmails. I think, why does someone want to talk to me but not connect with me? Aha, because they want to sell to me!

The numbers game may have worked in the past, but now on LinkedIn it is a waste of time. I always say that The Wolf of Wall Street and Del Boy are not welcome on LinkedIn! Yes, we're on LinkedIn to get business which means that we want people to 'buy our stuff' but if that is the only message we have, we won't get far. People want to know who they're buying from. People are less happy being sold to than ever before. We still want to buy, but we want to do so from people and companies that we trust.

Companies need to build that trust among their potential clients and customers, and using social selling on LinkedIn is one really powerful way of doing that.

Deals that start on social media platforms like LinkedIn have a higher chance of successfully being closed. In fact, according to LinkedIn Sales Solutions data:

💡 **78% of businesses that use social selling outsell businesses that don't use social media**[38]

Social selling is exactly what it says; using our social networks to build relationships with a view to gaining leads to sales. It is no surprise that LinkedIn is the primary social platform for B2B lead generation. LinkedIn is the only platform where you will find CEOs, CFOs and other C-Suite members openly communicating and sharing information.

Using LinkedIn, we can find out so much about people before we approach them. We can work out if someone is in need of our offering before we even say 'hello'. We can save ourselves, and others, a lot of time. No more 'cold calling'; using social selling effectively we start small, getting to know our potential leads before even introducing ourselves.

Finding prospective clients

On LinkedIn, growth is exponential. The more your network grows, the greater the potential your network has to grow even more. If everyone you connect with on LinkedIn can introduce you to, say, three more people, the road to expansion is limitless. It can look like a daunting task at first to expand your network, but start slowly and you will see your network grow and grow. Remember the analogy of picking blackberries - soon enough you will have a full basket, even one which is overflowing!

Building a network on LinkedIn should be a multi-pronged attack. I talked in chapter 4 about who a company should target; potential, current and previous customers, suppliers and collaborators, competitors, and influencers in the same industry. However, when it comes to developing a social selling strategy - converting connections into customers - we must hone in on finding good quality leads before we can begin building relationships and FINALLY turning them into sales prospects.

Those leads can be found in many ways on LinkedIn using different strategies.

1. By creating engaging and relevant content for people in our networks and also those who aren't
2. By proactively using the search tool to find people to introduce ourselves to
3. By using our existing followers and connections, asking them for referrals or by commenting on their posts

I have already covered content strategies and how to build a larger following through engagement. Now, let's focus on search and outreach.

Using the LinkedIn search tool to find leads

In this chapter, I introduce you to a valuable part of LinkedIn: the search option. When people realise the unleashed potential behind the 'search' box at the top of profiles, they quickly become devoted fans of LinkedIn and radically change their practices almost overnight!

When I get to this part in a company workshop, people have said 'THAT's what LinkedIn is for!' and 'NOW I get what the fuss is about.' That's when you know they'll be onboard, not only for outreach via LinkedIn but for increasing their personal following and the employee advocacy programme as a whole. This is the moment they realise they don't have to spend hours driving along motorways and staying in hotels and motels. They can sit at home in their PJs making connections and sales!

Using the LinkedIn search tool, it's possible to find people by sector, seniority, company, where they live, and so many more filters. Behind that search bar is a real treasure trove - so use it!

Using the search bar can be fiddly and take a bit of time at first, but it gets easier with practice and familiarity, and the searches get faster and more efficient.

> **When using the search option on LinkedIn, I advise starting with either a search for 'people' or 'companies'**

The best way to start is to put your cursor into the search bar and hit 'return'. The next step is to click the tab which says 'all filters' and fill in the sections. Start filling in one or two and see how many results that search shows. If that is too many people, use the other filters to narrow down your search until you have a manageable amount of people to connect with.

The next step is a great hack so don't miss this one! Unless your company has invested in Sales Navigator, you may think you can't save your searches and that you need to re-input your information each time you come to LinkedIn.

Read on, dear reader!

In order to save the search, simply save the URL of that search into your bookmarks. Then when you want to do some more searching, simply paste the URL back into your browser! Any 'new additions' to the search will come into the search too! Bingo.

Don't underestimate the power of LinkedIn search. I can't emphasise enough how easy it is to use and how much value it can bring you once you have the hang of it.

So, you've now got a list of people who you want to connect with, who are either relevant leads or who can get you in front of relevant leads. What next?

How to connect with a stranger

Many people really struggle with connecting on LinkedIn. I get it. It can seem a bit weird sending a connection request to someone we don't know - but that's what LinkedIn is for!

Receiving connection requests from a stranger on LinkedIn isn't as odd as it sounds. As long as that stranger introduces themselves.

> **Think of LinkedIn being the biggest networking party in the world. If no-one came up to us and introduced themselves while we're at that party, it would seem very strange, don't you think?**

As I said, employee advocacy is a multi-pronged approach. Each advocate should ensure that they have a concrete target of new connections to aim for, besides their regular sales targets. This will help them embrace this new strategy of growing their own networks and therefore the networks of the company.

If each advocate connects with three new people a week, this is a tangible, and achievable target which will drive more traffic to the company page and increase the company's brand voice right across LinkedIn, as well as helping that person to become a recognised thought leader in their field.

Growing our networks by three connections a week can be achieved without the need to invest in LinkedIn Premium. It's possible to grow your network by joining relevant groups, following companies in the industry and, of course, commenting on posts of people you're not connected to in the hope they instigate the connection request.

Once a target has been identified, the next step is to check out their profile, hit connect, add a personal note - this is essential - and hit 'send'.

Checking out someone's profile will help identify firstly if it's a fake profile (they do appear from time to time), and also that the person is a relevant connection. Not every new connection has to be a direct prospect. Think about those people who can help you take a step towards potential prospects. If, let's say, actors are a good prospect for you, then connections may include theatre and film directors and producers; or if you provide training to corporates, think of other people who also provide this service and find out how they get into certain organisations. You never know, you may get an introduction.

Knowing a bit about someone from their profile will also give the potential connector something to talk about when they send the request. Adding a note is not only a polite thing to do. It will help the message stand out among all the anonymous connection requests and, done correctly, will make it a no-brainer for your target to accept the request. Too many people go on a 'connect' spree and hope that some of the people will accept their request. It rarely works and it certainly doesn't help build a relationship.

> **It's better to spend time personalising a smaller number of requests than relying on 'spray and pray' methods**

There are various approaches to adopt when it comes to what the note should say:

1. Look for commonalities such as: lived in the same place, worked in the same sector, went to the same school or college (even if at different times)
2. Look for mutual connections - 'oh I see you know X person too....'
3. Is there something quirky about their banner or something they've said in their profile which you could mention or ask them about?
4. What have they, or their company, posted about recently? What are they interested in or focused on right now?

Whatever you do, do not sell! 'Selling' in a connection request is one sure fire way to be turned down. This first connection request is simply to get that connection in order to begin the relationship.

Once the request has been accepted, still do not sell! Keep building the relationship and, when the other party is ready, they will ask. If they don't, tread carefully and find the right time to start a gentle sales process.

Segment the teams

It would be a waste of resources to encourage multiple employees to look for the same categories of people. Divide and conquer! Once the advocates have been taught how to use this system and they feel comfortable using it, give each team, department or employee their own target audience to find.

These could be categorised in terms of:

1. Interests according to their activity on LinkedIn
2. Seniority in the organisation
3. Geography
4. Job role

For example, the tech team could engage with other tech people and potential customers who are keen to understand more about the tech side of the product.

Junior members of the team could start engaging with fellow juniors in other companies, 'warming them up' to get an introduction to the CEO for their CEO.

There are so many ways this can be managed, and the potential is enormous.

Continuing the relationships

Now that everyone knows how to find relevant people on LinkedIn, and they know how to send initial connection requests, the next thing is to encourage employees to engage in conversation so these new connections become relationships.

Posting regular content will help keep that brand awareness alive. However, with a focused content and engagement strategy, we are relying on the algorithm placing our content in the right people's feeds at the right time.

It is possible to adopt a more proactive approach and have a higher chance of staying in someone's thoughts as well as being able to position ourselves as the thought leader they want to see. Here, I offer two ways to do that.

1. Commenting on their posts
2. Getting a referral, aka 'the stealth approach'

1. Commenting on someone's posts

By 'popping up' in someone's feed every now and again, a person will remain top of mind. A good relationship is built on reciprocity. Giving something - advice, support or something tangible - helps build trust and cement a relationship. Helping someone gain more eyes on your content and positioning yourself as a thought leader or an expert in your field, can all be done easily without looking like you're showing off.

Make it your goal to make the conversation so interesting that even more people will comment

A well-placed and well-structured comment on someone else's post can be worth far more than the best performing post you have ever written. If you find a post written by someone in your network where you could add value in the comments, then don't be afraid to do so!

Apart from deepening the relationship with the person who has posted, the person who comments will also put themselves in front of the audience of that person. But first and foremost, the person who created the post will appreciate the contribution, and when this happens repeatedly they will start noticing the name of the person commenting. This is step one to building what could be a long lasting business relationship.

The importance of the trust we build through those conversations is crucial when we're not meeting each other face to face. As we're getting used to navigating and building relationships virtually, there are no limitations as to how far we can expand our reach and our business opportunities. This different approach is something we need to learn. For many people this is a new skill.

We need to take time to build and nurture relationships before even thinking about selling

TRUE STORY:

I had been working with 'Chris' to build his profile, which showed his journey from lawyer to executive business coach. I had encouraged him to write an introductory post about his new career, explaining to his audience what he was now doing.

Chris was a studious client and wanted to succeed on LinkedIn, but he was very nervous to comment on other people's posts. I saw a post by 'Anne' that I thought he should comment on and I encouraged him to do so using the strategy which I teach all my clients (this is outlined later in this chapter).

Chris took my instruction and commented on Anne's post. One of Anne's connections; 'Jane' saw Chris' comment and remembered him from when they worked together as lawyers. She checked out Chris' newly positioned profile and also read his introductory post. Jane, who was a follower of Anne's, was impressed, and thought to herself that Chris was ideally placed to speak at her conference for lawyers. She sent him a connection request reminding Chris who she was.

Chris replied, and they started to chat. A month later, Anne was flying Chris out to Istanbul to speak at a conference, for which she paid him a four figure sum.
All because of one comment on someone else's post. This stuff really works!

For a comment to be effective it needs thought and structure. It's no use just adding a few words of support or praise. When commenting on someone's post, think of it as just as important as creating your own original post. On LinkedIn, people read comments on posts and these can become separate conversations.

I can't say enough how powerful it is to add value when commenting on other people's posts, and the first rule is to think about your comment as if you were in a real life situation. Imagine yourself at a networking meeting standing around in a group, and one person leads the conversation with an interesting remark. Equate this to the 'post' before you comment. Think how you would respond to that remark if you were face to face.

In order to help you comment effectively, I would like to share with you my structure called '**The 4 C's of commenting**':

1. **Compliment**
   Who doesn't love a compliment? Beginning with a compliment will pretty much guarantee that the owner of the post will read it!

2. **Comment with value**
   Here you add your thought leadership or opinion - without showing off.

3. **Conversation**
   Use open language and encourage a conversation to happen between you, the owner of the post and anyone else around. This will help begin to build the relationship which you can nurture and build further over time.

4. **Connect**
   If you're not already connected to the post creator, head over to their profile and send a connection request. Add a note telling them how much you

enjoyed their post and that you would like to connect to know more about them.

Ta dah! If this system is rolled out in manageable, bite-sized chunks to all employees, think of the impact this could have on the company, even if just five people comment on one post a day.

The problem here can be knowing when someone has posted. We can trawl through our feeds but, unless we have very few connections, we don't see all the content that our connections post. So, without going to someone's profile and checking in on them, how do we know when a potential lead has posted?

The LinkedIn bell

Beneath the banner of anyone that you follow, you will see a bell icon. If you press - or 'ring' - that bell, it will become grey and you will now get a notification to tell you when that person posts. It really is a powerful tool and can save you lots of time trawling your feed. When you get the notification that the person has posted, the link to the post appears too - simple! Now all you have to do is comment on that post, using the 4C's method above. They don't know you've 'rung their bell' either so you're safe from looking like a stalker!

2. The stealth approach

Ok, let's look at a scenario where a CEO was identified as a potential lead on LinkedIn. However, you also learn that the CEO doesn't post on LinkedIn, nor comment on anyone else's posts so there is nothing to comment on. There is no apparent way to build that relationship further unless you keep sending them DM's. If s/he doesn't respond to those either, you will end up just looking spammy. I hear this all the time, it can be very frustrating.

What other options are there to get in front of that person?

See if you have a mutual connection. If yes, can you ask that person to give you a referral?

OR

Use someone else in the same company to 'leap frog' you there. Choose someone more junior than yourself initially. Befriend them, get their trust. Then ask them for an introduction to their line manager or someone more senior - but maybe not the CEO at this stage.

THEN

Build a relationship with this next person. They will be open to receive you as you have come via a recommendation from their colleague. Build on that relationship until you feel confident to ask for a referral to the CEO.

There you go, no pitching required! Patience and generosity are your best friends in social selling! That CEO may well want to check you out before they give you their time - even if you've come via a referral from one of their trusted team. If you have a fully completed profile and you're active on LinkedIn, that CEO may be more inclined to talk to you.

TRUE STORY

Alan was still at university studying IT when he joined one of my LinkedIn challenges. I was very impressed by this young man who realised how LinkedIn could help him get his first job when he graduated. He knew the company he wanted to work for and he wanted to adopt a very targeted approach.

Alan was aware that a CEO was unlikely to spend time communicating with him, he was 'only' an undergraduate. I advised him to start talking to a person he felt would accept his connection request; we identified the intern. The intern then (on request) recommended my young client to someone in the IT department.
After two weeks of his first communication with this company, the CEO sent Alan a DM asking him to come for an interview. He was hired on the spot!

This stuff works!

PART 4

MAXIMISING THE INVESTMENT

When I've given a company a one-off day of training, the whole team is on fire by the time I leave! Everyone is excited by their new, on brand, fully optimised shiny profile, they've created and posted a piece of interesting and engaging content and they've commented on each others' posts. Everyone has also found and messaged at least three new leads. Some have even had responses from those leads and got meetings booked in for the week ahead!

My workshops are fun, and I don't leave until I see that big progress has been made.

BUT…

Unless there is a structure or a process in place, all that energy and excitement will eventually perish. Without proper care, attention and follow up, it will be like joining the gym in January. After a couple of weeks, it all starts to tail off and after a while, the company's investment is pretty much wasted. The employees will look back on the day of training as valuable and interesting, but will not be taking action. This is why I talk about creating a SYSTEM of employee advocacy.

A company which gets positive results on a LinkedIn training day and then doesn't continue their activity is almost guaranteed to be losing out on potential income

CHAPTER 11

Steps to ensure the success of the programme

The employee advocacy programme, as well as the company page and profiles, needs to be maintained. If we stop working out, we'll go back to being unfit and flabby. If we stop posting and engaging on LinkedIn, our connections and followers will forget about us. More importantly, our competitors will be the ones approaching, engaging with, and potentially doing business with those potential customers.

So what needs to be done to ensure that the investment of time and money doesn't go to waste? How can we ensure that the energy and excitement within our advocacy group persists, ensuring that by the end of the following week/month/year the system of employee advocacy is still going strong?

Give the programme its own identity

Giving the system its own identity - and giving the participants 'membership' of the new 'club' - will help spark conversation around it in the company. It will also help people realise the gravitas and importance of the system and place it as something which is here to stay, rather than being just a vanity or tick box project. It could even have its own name to further strengthen the idea of it being an exclusive place for people to join.

One of my clients has the image of a lightbulb as part of their branding. We sat together and decided to call each advocate a 'bulb' and we named them 'The Chandelier Group'. Each advocate is a bulb growing and also shining a light on the company across LinkedIn!

Record everyone's base analytics

Monitoring each person's analytics will help keep track of who is bringing in the most brand awareness. Unless a company is using an employee advocacy tool, they will have to be dependent on each employee to share their analytics, which can help with accountability and transparency.

Whether or not an employee advocacy tool is used, collecting the baseline data for all employees is a prerequisite to knowing the impact of the programme later on. This data should therefore be collected at the beginning of the programme. If no automated tracking system is implemented, it could be collected as part of the training. When new employees join the programme further down the line, don't forget to collect their base data too. Having data to compare is essential to understand the ROI.

See the next chapter for more details on what to measure and what those measurements mean.

Set clear expectations

As with any new system, clear expectations will help people identify what they're doing and will help create accountability. I've said before that no one should be made to feel under pressure to take part in the system but by teaching, encouraging and supporting employees, a culture could emerge where each person wants to participate and add their contribution.

Providing each participant with a simple guide of expectations will ensure they know what they're doing and will want to assist in keeping the system alive.

Set up a collaboration system

Having a dedicated platform to run this system will help different aspects of it and could make it easier for all participants. A platform which is designed to share content, give different resources to different 'teams', and measure people's performance will bring a level of not only simplicity but also accountability to all users. Keeping the system simple with everything in one place will encourage all participants to keep moving forwards.

Whether a company chooses to use a dedicated platform or if they use an existing system such as those mentioned in

Chapter 5, all ambassadors will need to understand how this system works and be comfortable using it before they proceed.

Give people permission

Adding a new task to an already busy day isn't easy but it is important for each employee to carve out time in their day to do this. For years, we've been discouraged from using social media at work so this is a real mind shift. Giving people a set time period of - say - 20 minutes in their day when they can engage on LinkedIn will help move this system forward, as it will help them get over the 'fear' of sitting on their phones in the office.

Get the C-Suite on board

To create real change in mindsets, the authorisation and inspiration needs to come from the top. If CEOs are using LinkedIn, that will encourage the employees to follow suit. For an office junior to get a positive public comment on their LinkedIn post from the CEO or other member of the executive team could be the thing that really drives them forward and creates a permanent shift in their behaviour.

If the CEO is the one to invite people to join the programme, it highlights the level of importance being placed on the programme. If it is to be taken seriously, it should be given the attention it deserves.

Start conversations in the office

For any new system to succeed, it needs to be incorporated into the company culture. Starting conversations about what's happening on LinkedIn around the office will keep the system alive and will help to 'normalise' it as part of the fabric of the company.

If people start talking about LinkedIn as if it were Netflix, encouraging conversations around posts or accounts to engage with, this will drive activity and progression. This may also encourage new participants who will begin to feel FOMO or realise that the system is easier and more fun than they thought.

Talking about how the company uses employee advocacy when interviewing potential employees will embed the idea into people's heads before they walk through the door on their first day. It will mean each new employee is more likely to embrace the system and incorporate it into their working day right from the start.

Recognise and reward activity

Any activity should be rewarded, however small. Even clicking 'like' on a post may be a big step for someone, so make sure this activity is praised. Congratulating someone for what they do, even if it seems relatively insignificant, will hopefully push them on to continue and increase their efforts - maybe even progress to commenting. Bear in mind some people will start small and, as their confidence grows and they see the return on their time investment, they may feel motivated to do more.

Gamification

A bit of healthy competition is not a bad thing and may just keep people pushing forward. A company which offers a monthly prize or bonus to the most engaged employee or the post that creates the most engagement could see a considerable uptake! It could simply be a notification rather than an actual prize or even a monetary reward. What this has the potential to do is create more opportunities for posting too as the gamification could be talked about in LinkedIn posts, congratulating the monthly winners!

Recognise and reward different skills

Employee advocacy involves many skills: communication, copywriting, content creation and photography, to name some of them. It can appeal to members of the company in different ways. Some employees may shine at creating their own posts, whereas others may discover a skill for lead generation, image creation or even video.

Whatever skills emerge as part of this process, they should be embraced and encouraged as much as possible!

Some employees will embrace this new way of communicating and will realise they have a natural affinity for it. They could be assigned official or informal roles of 'champions'.

Others will struggle in terms of ability, confidence and time. They could be the 'supporters' whose role it is to react to others' posts rather than create their own original content.

Assigning different roles to different people and teams will help everyone stay engaged. This will help sustain the programme and even help it to grow. Before you know it, the presence of the company on LinkedIn has grown without you really noticing!

Proactively support the advocates

Whoever is running the system should offer a supportive and nurturing role rather than being a strict disciplinarian. If people feel they are going to be reprimanded if they don't participate, this can evoke feelings of anger or frustration around the programme which may lead members to dismiss it. This may lead them to do it badly or not at all.

To support those struggling with engagement, what may make this easier is finding content from external sources and sharing it with them. Employees may not have time to scroll through LinkedIn to find posts to comment on, so having someone to do that for them could help facilitate the process. Offering an 'open door' policy and answering questions when they arise will help prevent delays and disinterest setting in.

Bear in mind that some people may prefer a more 'private' approach and perhaps reaching out in a DM may be a better strategy than using the group platform to communicate. A gentle nudge or 'check in' message may just be enough to keep someone active in the system.

Centralise content creation

There are various things which can be done which will encourage activity and make it easier for employees to contribute.

Defining roles and frequency for the centralised part of content creation can include:

- Sharing links to company page posts so the teams can engage with them in a timely manner. Perhaps even planning who should be given time to prepare conversation-starting responses.
- Suggesting topics for the teams to create and post on their profiles - possibly even also creating post variations to share.
- Sharing resources such as brand palette, hashtags, brand values and language to help people craft their copy will ensure some cohesion and may provide inspiration for participants. Be careful here, as what is important is that each person's personality must shine through at all times.
- Creating a library of images that people can use or teaching employees how to use a design tool like Canva to make posts visually appealing will help the less creative and those who simply don't have the time to create their own images.

To create ownership and genuine engagement in the project, invite different groups of employees to regularly brainstorm ideas and allow them to air any concerns, worries or struggles. This will help contribute to the success of the system as it will give them a degree of 'ownership' of it.

Create a manageable schedule

It is obviously important to take into consideration each person's commitments and responsibilities, and recognise that employee advocacy is a new part of peoples' working day. It's an 'add-on' and extra time will need to be found to do it. This is why I encourage people to give 20 minutes of their day to this, as a maximum starting point. This could be 20 minutes in one block or a few minutes here and there. How long does a kettle take to boil? A value-add comment could be written and posted during this time.

What could that structure look like for each employee?

DAILY ACTIVITY FOR EACH EMPLOYEE

> Check the company page or the portal to see if a post is going or has gone live that day. If 'YES', like it, comment on it and either share it to your personal profile or even better post it again, creating a new post on your personal profile. Please note: if the company expects posts to be copied and pasted into personal profiles, each employee will need access to the copy and the image.
> Check notifications to see if anyone has mentioned you in a post or if anyone whose bell you have rung has posted. If 'YES", head over to that post or mention and comment using the 4 C's process.
> Check if you have any DMs to reply to.
> If time, scroll through your feed, looking for relevant posts to comment on.

- Find one person to connect with and send a well crafted connection request. This could be batch-done once a week to your three to five people, depending how you prefer to work - just don't forget to do it!

ONCE A WEEK

- Check and record your metrics (see chapter 12).
- Check on the activity of any 'warm' leads and see if they need a DM or a comment on a post. Think of any ways that you can drive the relationship forward. Focus on no more than 10 leads at a time. Keep notes/add them to a CRM system or spreadsheet so you can keep an eye on them.

ONCE A MONTH

- Go through the CRM system or spreadsheet to ensure you haven't missed anyone. Cull or put more focus on anyone who is not engaging.
- Consider finding a way to get a referral from a recent client or even a colleague.
- Share your analytics with the project leader - you may even win a prize!
- Think about your activity in the month ahead - is there anything happening which you could post about, or which others in the company could be posting about. Are you going to an event? Is there going to be something happening in the news which is relevant to curate or talk about? New product range? Someone's birthday or work anniversary?
- Team meeting to discuss how the month went for all advocates and to look at the month ahead as a group.

ONCE A YEAR

- Update your profile photo.
- Read through your profile. Any updates needed there, new position in the company, new roles added to your current role?

CHAPTER 12

Measuring and monitoring success

The return on investment of a company's LinkedIn activity takes time to prove. If a company is using an employee advocacy tool, this should be able to track activity including click throughs to an article and/or to the company page or website.

With this data, it will be easier to work out figures such as, cost per lead, effectiveness of each post as well as each ambassador.

The KPI's for setting up a system of advocacy will vary from company to company. They may include the number of followers on the company page, the level of engagement on posts, number of inbound enquiries there have been, or whether the number of job applicants has increased. It may also help you see if the quality of those applicants has improved over time.

But it will be more difficult to see where leads are coming in from using LinkedIn alone. Whether or not a system is used, it's important to set interim KPIs to ensure the process is driven forward and not abandoned.

Personal profiles have a limited number of analytic measurements, but company pages have more. This means that, without using third party tools, we can't take a really deep dive into who is engaging with our personal profiles; but on the plus side, it keeps the process simple and more sustainable for busy employees.

I worry when my clients start to deeply analyse their analytics all the time. I would rather they spend their limited time being active on LinkedIn than looking at their metrics. Obviously we need to know what is working, but I urge any user not to get so bogged down by numbers that they lose sight of what they're doing and why.

Analytics on personal profiles

Encouraging all advocates to record their own baseline metrics every day or even once a week, will usually spur them on to take action. Keeping them accountable and comparing their metrics monthly should facilitate a healthy competition and accountability among the employees. I have mentioned that implementing a system of 'reward' may also drive employees forward to do more.

One of the things I particularly love about LinkedIn is how our analytics are so highly reactive to our behaviour. This can promote immediate action. When an employee sees their metrics going up, even by a small degree, they are often inspired to push harder to continue the upward trend. It's a bit like the runner whose time gets faster or the weight lifter lifting heavier and heavier weights. When there are spikes, maybe a higher number of new followers on a particular day, that information could spur them on even more.

If some of the numbers begin to drop, a quick look at what's been happening (or not happening!) over the previous week will help us identify what has caused that shift. Hopefully, this will encourage the user to take action to bring those numbers back up.

Even the small changes that we make on LinkedIn can have an almost immediate impact. If I see one of my numbers drop, spending an extra 10 minutes engaging in other people's content can reverse that trend the following day.

Luckily, LinkedIn has made it very simple to measure the most important metrics. With an initial look, we can only see our four key metrics - and they are very easy to find.

On a regular basis, I advise looking only at the main four metrics

We can delve a little deeper into these four metrics when we click through each initial figure as it is presented to us on our profiles. We can also look at the metrics on each of our posts if we want more insight into how they are performing.

But a word of warning: it's easy to get too bogged down by detail and then we can lose the energy we need to keep moving forward. Looking more deeply once a week, or even just once a month, is enough to let us know if our content is aligned to our ideal audience and also which posts are getting better reach and engagement.

> **If you'd like a super simple chart which you can fill out in less than a minute every single day, go to: https://bit.ly/3weUF0J**

Managers and employees involved in the programme must understand what the most important metrics are and how to interpret the numbers.

The key metrics to measure are:

- Followers and connections
- Search appearances
- Post impressions
- Profile views

1. Followers and connections

What is the difference between a follower and a connection? Only LinkedIn has this differentiation and it can seem confusing. The biggest difference is that it is possible to 'follow' somebody without them knowing you exist, whereas a connection is someone you make a decision to build a relationship with - it's a two way process which involves both parties wanting to connect with the other.

The system of 'following' on LinkedIn works in a similar way to following someone on Instagram or Facebook. You just click the 'follow' button and hey presto! What happens next is that the posts of that person will appear in your feed. A person only knows who is following them by taking a look at their follower list.

A 'connection' is different in that both parties are involved in the relationship. You send someone a connection request, it remains 'pending' until they accept it. When you're connected to someone, you both get each others' content in your feeds, you can DM each other and you can write testimonials for each other should you wish.

Connecting with someone is the first step to building a relationship with them. The slightly confusing thing is that once two people are connected, they're automatically following each other.

So why 'follow' someone?

If you know a person will never connect with you but you still want to see their content in your feed then 'follow' them. Someone like Richard Branson won't connect with me (I asked him, I'm still waiting....), so I follow Richard and I get his content in my feed.

Following someone is useful if you want to keep an eye on what someone is doing without alerting them to the fact that you're 'watching' them. For example, a competitor or a potential client. When you're following someone, you can also ring their bell to get a notification when they post.

As mentioned, when two people are connected to each other, they're also following each other. But not the other way around. For this reason, you may see that your connection numbers are slightly lower than your number of followers. This is why we track follower numbers rather than connections.

Followers is a more accurate number than connections for how many people we are impacting with our content

2. Search appearances

We achieve a 'search appearance' when we appear in someone's key word search - when someone has used the 'search' option on LinkedIn and typed in one of the words or phrases we have in our profile.

This is why it's important to use the correct keywords and key phrases in our profiles - and also our posts. It is a bit of an anomaly though, as we may be in the top 3 shown to the person, or we may be number 264! This would be like

150

appearing on page 8 of a Google search - not much use at all! However, it's still an important figure to track and it still helps us see if what we're doing is working.

This statistic changes once a week and remains the same for seven days.

3. Post impressions

Post impressions are literally how many times your posts have appeared in other people's feeds. The measurement period is seven days and the number is updated daily.

Please be aware that an 'impression' does not mean that someone has 'read' the post. If a post has appeared in someone's feed, that counts as an 'impression'. The 'viewer' may have scrolled right past the post and not even noticed it was there. For more detailed analysis of how many people have actually seen the post, you'll need to go to the metrics on each post.

If you see your post impressions going down, take a look at what, and how many times, you have posted during the past week. In short, the more we post and the better quality our posts, the higher our post impressions will be.

All our posts should be appealing to our target audience. Watching the impressions and engagement on our posts is a very effective way to know whether we're doing it right or not.

If we have high post impressions but low engagement, it's worth thinking how we can get those people to participate in our content. Perhaps adding a poll would get the conversations started or asking a question in our posts?

4. Profile views

Profile views is the most important metric of all. A profile view is when somebody has taken action and visited our profile.

This can happen in several ways:

1. When we've met someone in person or online and given them our LinkedIn profile URL, or they've scanned our QR code. This will take them directly to our profile.
2. When someone has heard of us via someone else, or seen our name somewhere, and they've gone to LinkedIn and typed in our name. This will take them to our profile.
3. If we have our profile URL on our email footer or on our website (which I strongly advise you do), and someone has clicked through from there to your profile.
4. If someone has seen a post of ours in their feed which they found interesting, they may have clicked on our name which will take them to our profile.
5. If we've commented on someone else's post and a follower of that person likes our comment and has clicked through to our profile to find out more about us.
6. If someone has correctly tagged us in a post, it's easy for their followers to click through to see our profile.

The reason why this is the most important metric is because somebody has taken action to get to our profile. They actively want to know more about us. THIS is the metric you want to see going up and up. The period of measurement is 90 days, and the number changes daily.

If we're less active on LinkedIn over a period of time, we will see this number going down. However, the minute we post a valuable or interesting piece of content, or we start commenting on other people's posts, it's highly likely that we will see the number going up again. This is the metric which is going to spur your team on to be more active on LinkedIn.

This number is also likely to go up if you've been to an event and connected with a whole group of people.

Remember, LinkedIn is about growing our networks so, although it can be a lovely ego boost to get a whole load of new followers and profile views, it isn't just about the numbers.

Be strategic about who you connect with to ensure that you're building the RIGHT audience

Analytics on the company page

We are all aware that engagement on company pages is far lower than that of personal profiles - however, it's still important to know who is visiting the page and when. This will help us hone our content and our messaging.

The good thing about company pages is that the analytics go much deeper than on personal profiles. It's relatively easy to read quite detailed information about those people who are watching and absorbing our company page posts, even if they're not actively reacting to, commenting on, or sharing our posts.

Despite the depth of information provided, the analytics on a company page are fairly easy to read. It's also relatively straightforward to toggle between different timelines and areas of measurement.

The analytics are positioned very clearly in the menu on the left hand side of the page. What I like about company page analytics is that they are presented pictorially. This means it is easier to compare from day to day/week to week, etc. It's also easier to see spikes of activity. These are definitely worth delving into as they indicate some change on the page. This could be a change worth repeating.

There are a lot of 'lurkers' on LinkedIn: people who scroll, read and watch content but who don't engage with any posts. They're looking for things which grab their attention and, believe me, they will reach out if their interest is piqued or if they see something or someone they think can help them.

It's also possible to download the metrics into a pdf document. I recommend doing this reasonably regularly, as it's only possible to view our metrics for the previous year and not prior to that. It's important for a company to be able to make year on year comparisons. Comparing analytics before a system of employee advocacy is implemented is vital to tell a company whether or not the system is worth its investment.

If a company is using a tool to measure its advocacy programme, the tool will have its own metrics; however I think it is still important to closely monitor the LinkedIn metrics in case the company decides to switch platforms or stop using one altogether and rely on LinkedIn 100% to measure its success.

The point of gathering data is not just for fun, but to react to it.

I advise choosing one admin to collate the analytics and present them to the company in detail on a monthly basis.

So what are the measurements on a company page?

1. Content Highlights

> **Pages that post at least once a week see 5x more followers[39]**

There are so many factors which contribute to the success of individual posts. It is therefore important that one person is in charge of this process, as they are more likely to spot trends. That person needs time to see what is working and what is not working so well. I advise allowing at least three months of a new system to see how it is behaving.

Make sure that any changes that need to be made ARE made. This could include such things as:

- The level of engagement on posts, as well as the timing and type of engagement
- Using more (or less) photography over infographics or other types of image
- The style of content posted (polls, documents, etc)
- The level of involvement of staff in posts
- Changing the colours used in images
- Changing the length of posts
- Using more (or less) images
- Using more (or less) video
- Day and time of posting
- Hashtags used
- Tone of voice

The analytics on company page posts give a detailed picture of what is happening and who is engaging.

As well as being able to see the number of reactions, comments and reposts, it's also possible to see the difference between unique impressions vs total impressions, total engagement rate, and even click through rate - which shows a high level of engagement.

2. Visitor Highlights

Knowing who is visiting your page is really key information.

It's possible to compare visitors by how they visit, whether by desktop or by mobile, and also by job function, company size, industry, location or even their seniority.

Don't waste the golden opportunity that LinkedIn offers for you to find out about your audience!

Having a high number of page followers is something to aspire to, and in fact we believe LinkedIn favours pages with over 500 followers. However, what is important is to ensure that those followers are from the right industries and have the correct status and position in their organisations. If the demographic doesn't fit your ideal audience then look at things such as:

> - Design of the page
> - Outreach from the page
> - Content being published
> - Messaging and keywords
> - Who you're inviting to follow the page

Playing around with these criteria in a focused way will start to create a shift in who those visitors and followers are.

3. Follower Highlights

The same demographics are available for page followers so again, don't forget to use this information to ensure that your page and your content are appealing to the people you are trying to sell to.

It's a good idea to thank each follower when they do come along and follow the page, and keep in touch with them via some of the team's personal profiles too. This way you can capitalise on the fact that they are obviously interested in what the company has to say.

Don't forget that it's possible to invite people to follow the page every single month which gives you a level of control over the types of followers. Use this opportunity wisely!

4. Lead Highlights

These are the people who have completed the 'lead gen form'. It is possible to use lead gen forms to collect quality leads from members who visit the LinkedIn page or Showcase page. It is easier for visitors to the page to complete a partially pre-filled form and click 'submit' than to follow a link which takes them off the LinkedIn platform to fill out a form.

The problem with lead gen forms is that the admins don't get notified when one has been completed. In order to manage the expectations of visitors to the company page, if the form is switched on, ensure someone checks every day to see if a form has been submitted. A more advanced strategy is to use a third party app like Zapier. This will set up automated workflows to take the next step with the person and bring them into a sales funnel or add them to an email newsletter. Don't leave money on the table, folks! Make it easy for a visitor to take that next step.

5. Newsletter Highlights

If a company has the resources to publish a regular (monthly, bi-weekly or weekly) newsletter, I strongly advise that they do so. There is a caveat here in that it's a good idea to build up the following on the page before publishing the first newsletter. I recommend waiting until there are at least 1000 relevant followers. The reasons for this are not straightforward and fall outside the parameters of this book. Please get in touch if you'd like to know more.

As with newsletters published via personal profiles, it is possible to see who is subscribed to the company newsletter. If a person has taken action to subscribe to the company's long form content, they are a warm lead! They are prepared to invest their time to find out more about the company.

All employees should be notified of subscribers to the company newsletter to give them the chance to build a personal relationship with them. Reaching out to say 'I see you have subscribed to the company newsletter, do you have any questions we can answer for you?' is a positive step which shows a company is interested in its audience. Can you imagine the impact of a CEO reaching out and saying that to a newsletter subscriber? That would be really powerful and can be done in a matter of seconds!

6. Competitor Highlights

This is a feature I really like on LinkedIn company pages and I haven't seen it on any other platform, ever! It's possible to monitor the success of your competitors and compare your figures to theirs. Being able to see what your competitors are up to and how well their posts are performing can be highly valuable so don't underestimate the importance of these analytics.

Choose your 10 competitors wisely but bear in mind you can change them at any time. Keeping an eye on what they're doing will give a company an insight into whether their LinkedIn activity is successful. I advise any company to check out the actual pages and posts of competitors to really keep an eye on this and see if they can get to, and stay at, the top of the list!

LinkedIn looks at the number of posts on your page compared to your competitors, and the total engagement rate on the page. It then shows you any 'trending posts' from your competitors. All this can be really useful when you're thinking of what and how to post.

7. Search highlights - available on mobile only

Similar to search in personal profiles, this is measuring the number of times a page comes up in a LinkedIn search. Posting regularly on the page is one way to help this figure go up. Using relevant keywords and phrases will be instrumental too, of course. Don't dismiss the importance of using key phrases and keywords when setting up the page to help come up in searches on LinkedIn as well as on Google.

The End - or is this the beginning?

If you're a business owner, I urge you not to just close the cover of this book and put it on your shelf. I am asking you to really think about what you've read and take a look at your business development and your marketing in a new light. Ask yourself if some sort of employee advocacy programme could work for your company. Do you have employees who you feel could go out on LinkedIn and begin positioning themselves as thought leaders - for their own gain and also to help the efforts of the company? Could some of your team members spend just 20 minutes a day on LinkedIn to potentially make a big shift in sales for your company?

Take a look at your company page with fresh eyes and ask yourself if it truly represents what happens in your organisation. Look at the page itself as well as the content. Is it just a mini version of your website, or does it do something different? Does it show the heart of your organisation, the personalities within it?

If you're an employee, would it be worth recommending this book to your boss?

Closing note

I joined LinkedIn on December 1st 2015. I had no followers and no connections and I didn't even post on the platform for about a year!

My first post generated an inquiry which won me my first LinkedIn training client, and my second post also led to a client. I realised there was something to leverage here, so I investigated further. I've since built a successful business by posting and commenting on LinkedIn. No ads, no salesy spam. Just pure, organic marketing. LinkedIn really does work to generate leads to grow businesses.

Would you ask someone to marry you on a first date? Growth on LinkedIn doesn't happen quickly - but LinkedIn growth is exponential, followers attract followers. In 7 ½ years, I've built an engaged audience of over 17,000. I did all this on my own - I have had no employees to advocate my content. If I can do it on my own, what is stopping companies with employees doing it?

LinkedIn has changed enormously since I started posting - undoubtedly for the better. I urge you to jump on and join the ride! It'll be fun and, most importantly of all, it will be productive for you and your company if you do it the right way.

Of course, I'd be happy to advise and share my years of experience and learning with you. Just hop over to LinkedIn and send me a DM - it really is that easy!

Sarah

The story of this book & acknowledgements

Who knows where our lives will take us? The twists and turns which lead us to where we dwell are often unpredictable and unforeseen.

I started out wanting to be a lawyer, and now here I am helping business leaders with their personal branding and working with organisations to help them spread their message! It's been quite a journey and there are many people to thank who have helped me along the way. For this book in particular, the following people all need a mention.

Richard van der Blom for all your amazing knowledge and insights. John Espirian; for my first ever LinkedIn lesson and for always being 'relentlessly helpful'! Also for introducing me to some of my LinkedIn besties: Gillian Whitney, Jeff Young, Kevin D. Turner and Stella da Silva who, along with John, have supported me from the start and helped me build my tribe.

My husband for letting me escape at the weekends to focus on this book and listen while I try to explain how difficult this process is!

My kids for not laughing at me as I danced around the garden wearing nothing but my headphones and a swimsuit, hovering different coloured felt tips over large pieces of paper at the very beginning of this process.

Corinne McGee for being an eagle eyed proofreader, I hope you learned something!

Mic Adam for giving me your time, your support and encouragement and the validation I needed to actually send the manuscript to print.

Malene Bendtsen for your encouragement, your laughs, your unfailing support and your patience - which I know I have tested to its limits. You have stood by me and supported me throughout the whole process. I shared some of my deepest secrets with you - you have been my counsellor as well as my cattle prod, my advisor, editor, publisher and, above all, you have become a great friend.

All of my followers and connections on LinkedIn, who have helped me grow my business which has provided me not only with an income, but a life of joy and exciting challenges. You rock my world every single day - thank you!

About the author

Sarah Clay is an award-winning social media trainer and strategist, specialising in LinkedIn lead generation and brand awareness. She trains B2C and B2B companies and CEO's how to create their brands and make the most of LinkedIn. Offering a no-nonsense, accessible approach to her teaching, Sarah also manages to inject some fun into learning.

As a keynote speaker, Sarah delivers inspirational talks worldwide on subjects based around LinkedIn, personal branding and thought leadership.

Sarah is also a guest lecturer at several UK universities, helping the students establish themselves on LinkedIn to start their careers.

Sarah publishes a regular newsletter on LinkedIn and on her website, www.sarahclaysocial.com. She has been published in AgoraPulse, Social Media Pulse, Brand You Magazine, HR Grapevine and Social Media Examiner and has appeared on numerous podcasts, lives, and radio shows.

References

[1] https://www.cendex.co.uk/resources/labour-turnover-rates

[2] https://business.linkedin.com/content/dam/me/business/en-us/elevate/Resources/pdf/official-guide-to-employee-advocacy-ebook.pdf

[3] https://sociuu.com/wp-content/uploads/2022/09/employee-advocacy-benchmark-2023.pdf

[4] *Chris Boudreaux, "The Most Powerful Brand on Earth" (2013)*

[5] https://hingemarketing.com/uploads/hinge-research-employee-advocacy.pdf

[6] https://www.slideshare.net/jaybaer/8-things-online-influencers-can-do-for-you#3

[7] https://www.edelman.com/trust/2023/trust-barometer

[8] https://www.mckinsey.com/capabilities/growth-marketing-and-sales/our-insights/the-consumer-decision-journey

[9] https://www.inlytics.io/post/linkedin-company-page-vs-personal-profile-which-one-should-you-use-in-2022

[10] https://www.krusecontrolinc.com/rule-of-7-how-social-media-crushes-old-school-marketing-2021

[11] https://www.linkedin.com/pulse/give-me-straight-does-google-index-linkedin-articles/

[12] https://faculty.wharton.upenn.edu/wp-content/uploads/2012/04/Schmitt-Skiera-vandenBulte-2011-Referral-Programs-Customer-Value.pdf

[13] https://sociuu.com/wp-content/uploads/2022/09/employee-advocacy-benchmark-2023.pdf

[14] https://thesocialshepherd.com/blog/linkedin-statistics

[15] https://www.techtarget.com/searchhrsoftware/definition/passive-candidate

[16] https://www.centrichr.co.uk/what-is-the-true-cost-of-replacing-an-employee

[17] https://www.robertwaldinger.com/

[18] https://www.wellsteps.com/blog/2022/05/17/happy-employees-more-productive

[19] https://quotefancy.com/quote/898907/Richard-Branson-Create-the-kind-of-workplace-and-company-culture-that-will-attract-great

[20] https://www.enterpriseappstoday.com/stats/social-media-at-workplace-statistics.html

[21] https://info.culture.io/hubfs/CulturePartners_Research Series_CultureStrength.pdf

[22] https://www.wtwco.com/en-gb/insights/2021/10/how-employers-can-move-from-the-great-resignation-to-the-great-retention

[23] https://www.pushfar.com/article/unlocking-employee-potential-the-awesome-benefits-of-employee-upskilling

[24] https://www.cnbc.com/2018/11/13/why-work-friendships-are-critical-for-long-term-happiness.html

[25] https://journals.sagepub.com/doi/abs/10.1177/0021886318 773459

[26] https://www.headspacegroup.co.uk/should-you-celebrate-birthdays-in-the-workplace

[27] https://www.tinypulse.com/blog/17-surprising-statistics-about-employee-retention

[28] https://business.linkedin.com/marketing-solutions/linkedin-pages/best-practices#1

[29] https://www.socialstatus.io/insights/social-media-benchmarks/linkedin-organic-reach-rate-benchmark

[30] https://business.linkedin.com/marketing-solutions/linkedin-pages/best-practices#1

[31] https://blog.hubspot.com/marketing/how-frequently-should-i-publish-on-social-media

[32] https://www.youtube.com/watch?v=sKtBkVrqYYk

[33] https://jamesclear.com/new-habit

[34] Unique Selling Point

[35] https://kinsta.com/blog/linkedin-statistics

[36] https://blog.hubspot.com/sales/hubspot-sales-strategy-report

[37] https://www.socialpilot.co/blog/linkedin-statistics

[38] https://business.linkedin.com/sales-solutions/social-selling

[39] www.linkedin.com

Printed in Great Britain
by Amazon